MW00989793

# YOU
# BELONG
# TO THE
# UNIVERSE

# YOU
# BELONG
# TO THE
# UNIVERSE

BUCKMINSTER

FULLER AND

THE FUTURE

JONATHON
KEATS

OXFORD
UNIVERSITY PRESS

# OXFORD
UNIVERSITY PRESS

Oxford University Press is a department of the University of Oxford. It furthers
the University's objective of excellence in research, scholarship, and education
by publishing worldwide. Oxford is a registered trade mark of Oxford University
Press in the UK and certain other countries.

Published in the United States of America by Oxford University Press
198 Madison Avenue, New York, NY 10016, United States of America.

© Jonathon Keats 2016

Library of Congress Cataloging-in-Publication Data
Keats, Jonathon, author.
You belong to the universe : buckminster fuller and the future / Jonathon Keats.
    pages cm
Includes bibliographical references and index.
ISBN 978-0-19-933823-8 (hardcover : alk. paper)    1. Fuller, R. Buckminster
(Richard Buckminster), 1895–1983.    2. Architects—United States—Biography.
3. Inventors—United States—Biography.    I. Title.
TA140.F9K43 2016
620.0092—dc23
[B]
2015030656

9 8 7 6 5 4 3 2 1
Printed by Sheridan, USA
Printed in the United States of America on acid-free paper

*For Silvia. Sempre, sempre.*

# CONTENTS

GUINEA PIG B     1

*The Buckminster Fuller Myth*     *1*

HOW TO MAKE THE WORLD WORK     27

*Six Visions*     *27*

1. Mobility: The Dymaxion Car     29

2. Shelter: The Wichita House     47

3. Education: Two-Way TV     70

4. Planning: The Geoscope     93

5. Environment: The Dome Over Manhattan     115

6. Peace: The World Game     134

THE RANDOM ELEMENT     163

*The Buckminster Fuller Legacy*     *163*

*Further Reading*     *191*

*Index*     *193*

# YOU
# BELONG
# TO THE
# UNIVERSE

# GUINEA PIG B

*The
Buckminster
Fuller
Myth*

# I   Epiphany

LATE ONE EVENING in the winter of 1927, Buckminster Fuller set out to kill himself in frigid Lake Michigan. At thirty-two years old, he was a failure. He had neither job prospects nor savings, and his wife had just given birth to a daughter. A life insurance policy, bought while he was in the Navy, was all that he had to support his family.

So Fuller walked down to a deserted stretch of shoreline on the North Side of Chicago. He looked out over the churning water and calculated how long he'd need to swim before succumbing to hypothermia. But as he prepared to jump, he felt a strange resistance, as if he were being lifted, and he heard a stern voice inside his head: "You do not have the right to eliminate yourself. You do not belong to you. You belong to the universe." Then the voice confided that his life had a purpose, which could be fulfilled only by sharing his mind with the world, and that his family would always be provided for, as long as he submitted to his calling.

He went home and told his wife. He explained that he no longer needed a job. He said that he had to think, and would not utter a word until he knew what he truly thought. For two full years, Fuller was silent. He filled five thousand pages with notes, as if in a trance. His jottings and sketches revealed the secret to making the whole human race successful for all eternity. He spent the rest of his life openly sharing the secret with everybody.

At least that's how he later characterized his 1927 trans-formation, addressing lecture halls crowded with disciples listening to his wisdom for seven or eight hours at a stretch. Sometimes he changed details, such as whether his daughter was born before or after his lakeside epiphany, or the number of years he was silent, or how many pages he'd written. In interviews he might embellish his tale, claiming that he'd slept just two hours each night, or had become a vegetarian, or had moved his family into a slum where the neighbor was an Al Capone henchmen. Such details could easily be adjusted because even the essentials of his tale were essentially invented.

Scrutinizing the copious records he kept of his life—a 45-ton archive that he dubbed the Dymaxion Chronofile—scholars have found no evidence of a suicide attempt, or even a change in diet.[1] Fuller did lose his job shortly after his daughter was born, but he found work within months. He became an asbestos flooring salesman, hardly a silent profession. Nonetheless, his files contain hundreds of pages of notes from the late 1920s, and the notes show that he was conceiving the philosophy and technology that would later mark his career as a self-proclaimed comprehensive anticipatory design scientist. During this period—as he started lecturing, and self-published his first book—he also began the process of crafting a personal myth.

The myth became more elaborate with repetition. It also grew more important as a narrative that illustrated his ideas and revealed linkages, rendering his worldview more intelligible to the broad public he sought to convert. Given his ambition of making the entire human race successful for all eternity, comprehensive anticipatory design science

---

1. Now archived at Stanford University, the Chronofile is the most comprehensive record of an individual life known to exist. The Chronofile contains virtually every scrap of paper that related to Fuller, from his manuscripts and drawings to personal and professional correspondence to newspaper and magazine clippings. There are also a large number of unpaid bills and library citations for overdue books. Throughout his life, Fuller folded the Chronofile into his personal myth, alluding to it as evidence of his commitment to total autobiographical objectivity. Since his death, the Chronofile has ironically revealed how little of his life story conformed to fact.

necessarily drew on bodies of knowledge as disparate as architecture, cartography, biology, economics, and cosmology. His life story helped to unify these fields for his audience.

And also for himself. Every time he recounted his myth, Fuller reformulated his vision, combining his ideas differently with each variation. Self-mythologizing was his way of thinking. Autobiographical fraudulence afforded intellectual flexibility.

He was too priggish to admit it. He insisted that he was being completely forthright. Time and again, he advertised his openness by dramatically confessing his suicide attempt, and justified his candor by modestly describing himself as a human guinea pig. His life was "an experiment to discover what the little, penniless, unknown individual might be able to do effectively on behalf of all humanity."[2] The man who'd stood on the shore of Lake Michigan could have been anyone. Everybody could succeed as he had done, if only they embraced his beliefs and belonged to the universe.

For all the factual inaccuracies, Fuller's personal myth is his truest intellectual biography. Moreover, because there's no authoritative version—no consistency between tellings—his ideas remain as pliable today as when he was alive. His insights and innovations can be endlessly recombined and reimagined as global circumstances change. Revisiting his myth—with all its historical inaccuracies—is fundamental to reviving and renewing his thinking. For that reason, this book begins with a legend—foundational to the reconsideration of Fuller's ideas and innovations in the chapters that follow. And the legend begins in 1895, in the old Massachusetts town of Milton.

<hr />

2. He recited variations on this line whenever he was given a chance. Permutations appear in his books and newspaper accounts of his speeches. More succinctly, he broadcast the illusion of modesty by insisting that everyone call him *Bucky*, his nickname since childhood.

## II   The Myth

BUCKY FULLER WAS an ungainly child. One leg was shorter than the other. Unlike his sister, he was cross-eyed and astigmatic. She talked about things he couldn't see, so he thought she was kidding. Not to be outdone, he conjured his own imaginary beings.

The grown-ups caught on in kindergarten, when a teacher asked him to make a house out of dried peas and toothpicks. He did it by touch. Instead of making a box, he built a series of interlocking tetrahedra. Their sturdiness, he reckoned, must make them the basis of all architecture. The grown-ups tried to set him straight by correcting his eyesight.

But his glasses did nothing to change his perspective. He stubbornly trusted his own experience over what people said. Why build houses as flimsy cubes, guided by tradition, when trial and error showed the strength of tetrahedra? In fact, Bucky was baffled by most of what grown-ups believed. He was particularly mystified in math classes, where teachers talked in unfathomably abstract terms. He'd raise his hand when an instructor drew geometric figures on the blackboard. He'd ask what triangles were made of and how heavy squares were. He'd inquire about their temperature. His teachers accused him of insubordination, but his curiosity was perfectly earnest.

His only respite came in summer, when his family would move to an island they owned off the coast of Maine. Bear Island offered little more than rudimentary shelter. Wood was chopped by axe and water was drawn from a pump. The wood was weighty. The water was cold. Nothing on Bear Island was abstract.

Bucky thrived on physical labor, which included a daily voyage by dinghy to retrieve the family's mail. Making the circuit alone, he learned about tides and navigation. He also observed the life around him, which gave him the idea for his first invention: an oar loosely modeled on jellyfish propulsion. His mechanical jellyfish was constructed like an upsidedown umbrella at the end of a pole that slid through a loop at the back of his rowboat. Submerged in the water, the jellyfish opened when he pushed on it and closed as he pulled. It allowed him to cover good distance with little work. In a stroke, he saw that efficiency was a matter of design, and that nature had no tolerance of waste.

But invention wasn't something that a Fuller man did for a living. The Fullers of Milton were clergymen and lawyers. His father was a merchant. And when Richard Buckminster Fuller, Sr., died around Bucky's fifteenth birthday, Bucky's career path was settled. He would go to Harvard—as the previous four generations of Fuller men had done—and return to support his family.

Lest his obligations be lost on him, an uncle summoned Bucky for a talk. The old man said that the world worked on principles set down by the political economist Thomas Malthus in 1798: There wasn't nearly enough wealth for everybody to succeed, and resources would only become more scarce as the population inevitably increased. To thrive in society and preserve his family's status, Bucky must always keep the poor in their place.

But at Harvard, *he* felt impoverished. Most acquaintances from boarding school dropped him; with Malthusian cunning, they calculated that he had too little money to be admitted to a club, and his friendship would therefore diminish their chance of success. He tried out for the football team, and broke a kneecap. All social prospects shattered, he started skimping on schoolwork and going out at night, prowling the backstreets of Boston, accompanied by his sister's wolfhound.

The dog provided a ruse for Bucky to meet showgirls. He'd lead the exotic animal to the stage door of a cabaret, feigning wealth, prompting conversation. His most intense infatuation was with a starlet named Marilyn Miller. After courting her in Boston, he followed her to Manhattan, where he demonstrated his feelings by treating her whole chorus line to a champagne banquet. In a single evening, he blew more than his allowance for the year. He also, incidentally, missed freshman midterms.

That was cause for expulsion. Relatives bailed out his poor mother, and contrived a punishment for his disgraceful behavior. He was exiled to a factory town in rural Quebec to work at a textile mill.

Bucky scarcely noticed the dearth of pretty young women. Apprenticed as a machine fitter, he was finally getting an education. He worked long hours learning to assemble textile machinery shipped from France and England. Many of the British machines were defective. Shunning sleep, he spent his nights figuring out how they were supposed to work and designing new parts. His fixes often involved improvements. He did too well for his own benefit. Hearing about his diligence, relatives called him home and sent him back to Harvard.

The school saga repeated, albeit without Marilyn Miller or the wolfhound. Bucky skipped classes, got expelled, took a job, and recommended his experiential education. This time it was in meat packing, as an employee of Armour & Company. He worked the 3:00 AM to 5:00 PM shift six days a week, overseeing the transportation of meats from warehouse to market in New York. The logistical challenges enthralled him. So did refrigeration, a recent invention that minimized spoilage so that more people could eat well: a case of technology counteracting Malthusianism.

On his days off, Bucky liked to dance. At one party on Long Island, where his sister's family lived, he danced with a girl named Anne Hewlett. She was the daughter of a prominent New York architect, and had a family lineage nearly as distinguished as the Fullers. Since Bucky happened to be working in an Armour plant astride the Long Island Railroad, he started calling on her often. Each time he spent his wages on a bunch of roses. His generosity impressed her. They got engaged.

That was in the summer of 1916. Woodrow Wilson was running for re-election, campaigning on the promise that he'd keep America out of the war. Germany didn't care. U-boats threatened American lives. Bucky bristled with patriotism.

He was rejected by the Army on account of his eyesight. Lest the Navy also snub him, he offered his family's boat—a forty-foot cabin cruiser called the *Wego*—to patrol the Maine coastline. Since his was the first boat volunteered, they appointed him chief boatswain, and ordered him to watch the waters for submarines.

What he found was the geometry of the universe. Looking at the bubbles made by the *Wego*'s propellers, he recalled his boarding school math teachers, who had taught him to measure a sphere's volume in terms of *pi*. He also remembered that *pi* was an irrational number, a decimal that never ended. He asked himself how nature could ever make bubbles in such circumstances. Did nature approximate? The rules his teachers had taught him must be mistaken. Spheres ought to be understood in terms of the forces that made them. At the age of twenty-one, Bucky determined that the universe had no objects. Geometry described forces.

It was an insight bound to shape Bucky's entire worldview—informing every future invention—but he didn't have time to apply it just then. On April 6, 1917, the United States entered World War I. Two months later, Bucky married Anne. The *Wego* was retired. Bucky was sent to the Naval Academy in Annapolis for three months of intensive training.

The curriculum suited his talents and temperament. Naval officers were trained comprehensively so that they could operate anticipatorily if the chain of command was broken by conditions at sea. Recruits were taught geography and navigation. They learned logistics and ballistics and mechanics. Based on his technical aptitude, Bucky was made a communications officer in the Atlantic fleet. He assisted in pioneering radio experiments. Witnessing the first wireless communication between ship and plane, he grew convinced that all technology was accelerating, becoming increasingly effective and ubiquitous. Also ethereal. The radiotelephone could replace heavy cables. Alloys could make machinery lighter and stronger. Technology meant doing more with less. Progress was self-perpetuating. Knowledge was an infinitely renewable resource, rendering Malthusianism obsolete.

Or it could be if the world worked like the Navy. Resigning his commission after the armistice to be at home with his wife and infant daughter, Bucky was aghast at the technological gap between military and civilian life. He watched helplessly as his child succumbed to one illness after another. Alexandra suffered from influenza and pneumonia and spinal meningitis, all preventable, he believed, if housing were more sanitary. Her death at the age of four reinforced his conviction that technology needed to be domesticated—transferred from weaponry to "livingry."

His father-in-law had an idea. As an architect, James Monroe Hewlett was struck by the inefficiency of home construction. Everything was built on site, requiring the services of master carpenters and masons who worked in traditional materials. As a result, good housing wasn't widely available. Hewlett envisioned a building system that would be less expensive and easier to assemble: Bricks would be replaced with blocks of compressed woodchips braced with reinforced concrete. He brought in Bucky as a partner.

By 1927, Stockade Building Systems had supplied the materials for 240 houses. Bucky served as president, working fifteen hours a day, overseeing five regional offices. But investors were never satisfied with the profits, unable to appreciate the difficulty of Bucky's task: He had to overcome the resistance of the traditional building industry in every town and city. Finally the shareholders ousted him, the same month that his daughter Allegra was born. Bucky had no money, only his life insurance policy from the Navy. He set out to kill himself on Lake Michigan.

✦

IN HIS TWO years of silence, Bucky completely reconceived housing. This time there were no compressed woodchips. The house of the future would be made entirely of lightweight plastics and high-strength alloys, fabricated and assembled in a factory, air-delivered by zeppelin. Designed according to Bucky's geometric principles, it would hang from a mast, completely self-contained and perfectly balanced. It would be sanitary and efficient and inexpensive enough that anyone could own it. His 4D House would alleviate poverty, prevent disease, and allow the human race to thrive for the first time in history.

He secured a patent, and explained the underlying phi- *BK*
losophy in a fifty-page book called *4D Time Lock*. He mimeographed 200 copies. With his text and blueprints and an
architectural model, he headed to the American Institute of
Architects (AIA) convention in St. Louis, Missouri.

Bucky offered his house to the architects. He freely gave
all intellectual property rights—in keeping with his 1927
vow—so that the AIA could oversee global implementation
of his plan. They turned him down. Protective of their profession, threatened by mass-production, the architects unan-
imously passed a resolution opposing standardized housing.

He was more warmly received in Chicago. The Marshall
Field's department store was eager to sell modern furniture,
and Bucky's invention stunningly evoked the future. All that
was wanting was a catchy name. So the store hired a publi-
cist, who noted Bucky's favorite words: *dynamic, maximum,
tension.* The 4D House became the *Dymaxion.*

Bucky brought his Dymaxion house to Boston and
Manhattan, lecturing wherever he found an audience. He
talked at Harvard University and the Architectural League
of New York, and even at a Greenwich Village tavern called
Romany Marie's. Word spread. The American Standard
Sanitary Manufacturing Company contacted him, interested in producing his bathroom. He developed a prototype: an all-in-one steel unit that was light and efficient and
could be installed in any home without custom pipework.
Plumbers' unions were aghast. American Standard canceled
his project.

The experience was becoming all too familiar. It echoed
Bucky's misadventures at Stockade and with the AIA. He
remained convinced that technology could better people's
lives, but perceived that the entire building industry needed
reform. To reform it, Bucky needed a platform.

In 1932, he cashed in his life insurance, bought a publication called *T-square*, renamed it *Shelter*, and made it the most technologically progressive architectural journal in the United States. *Shelter* presented housing as an engineering problem. Ships and airplanes were shown as architectural paradigms. Articles promoted mass-production as an antidote to Depression-era squalor. Builders remained unpersuaded. *Shelter* went out of business. The only idea that survived: Dymaxion transportation.

Like the bathroom, it related to Dymaxion housing. As a comprehensivist, Bucky was concerned with all aspects of living. Since his homes were portable, he reasoned that future families might not live on roads. They'd need to get around by air. They'd want a flying car.

Bucky's car was to have inflatable wings, and it was designed for vertical takeoff on rotatable jets. Because the required materials didn't yet exist, he proposed to perfect ground taxiing first. He would make the world's first car to have the streamlining of an airplane. With capital from a stockbroker who'd seen his concept in *Shelter*, he opened a factory in Bridgeport, Connecticut, hiring twenty-seven workmen to build three experimental prototypes.

The Dymaxion car drove on three wheels, two in the front and one in the rear. The aluminum shell was shaped like an airship, enclosing seating for eleven people. With an eighty-five horsepower Ford engine, Bucky could surpass ninety miles per hour, with fuel efficiency of thirty miles per gallon. In other words, the car could travel at twice the speed of a Ford on half the fuel, carrying three times the number of people. Bucky could also steer the car on its own axis, pulling into a parking space without putting it in reverse. It was a triumph of design—a perfect demonstration of doing

more with less—impressing everyone from H. G. Wells to
Amelia Earhart.

And then there was an accident. At the Chicago World's
Fair, one of the prototypes was hit by another car. It rolled
over, killing the driver. The other vehicle belonged to a city
official, and was towed off before the media arrived. In newspapers the next morning, the deadly flip was attributed to
Bucky's radical design. The automotive industry—tepidly
interested in Bucky's concept—withdrew all support. Bucky's
company folded yet again.

But Bucky still wasn't discouraged. If anything, he was
beginning to see these serial failures as affirming. In all of
his misfortune, he detected a pattern: He was consistently
ahead of his time. His ideas were fit for the future. The most
he could ever do was to anticipate what would be needed.
In order to anticipate more accurately, he began a systematic
study of all the world's resources and human living requirements, and started to publish his findings. He considered the
world logistically, drawing on his experience at Armour and
his training in the Navy. He produced charts for *Fortune* magazine, and published a book called *Nine Chains to the Moon*.
In his writing, he approached invention as a convergence of
resources, capabilities, and needs, facilitated by design.

The convergence could occur in the least expected of set-
tings. Driving through Illinois in 1940, Bucky saw that farmers
stored their grain in cylindrical bins the size of small houses.
There was no reason that the metal containers couldn't be
fitted with windows and doors, becoming factory-deliverable
mass-produced single-family dwellings. As Bucky calculated
how to make the bins habitable, World War II made portable shelter essential. Thousands of his Dymaxion Deployment
Units were shipped overseas to house American soldiers.

And Bucky was summoned to Washington, D.C., appointed to the Board of Economic Warfare as chief mechanical engineer. He gave weekly briefings on global resources. To better understand their distribution, he developed his own cartographic projection that flattened the world without distortions. He dubbed it the Dymaxion Air-Ocean World Map, and developed versions showing raw materials and transportation routes.

Bucky was also responsible for monitoring domestic economic conditions. He observed the growing demand for housing as soldiers came home and started families. Building homes in factories no longer seemed as outlandish as it had in the 1920s, and factories needed work as the war subsided and fewer weapons were produced. Bucky's Dymaxion dwelling concept seemed apt to fill the gap. He proposed to fabricate housing at a Beech airplane plant in Wichita, Kansas. Beech readily agreed.

Bucky's new Dymaxion was made of aircraft aluminum. It was air-deliverable and could be assembled in a day without specialized labor. It had many of the advantages promised by the original house-on-a-mast, including cleanliness, climate control, and affordability, but was more practical because the essential technologies were already available. When prototypes were completed in 1945, the house attracted ten thousand pre-orders. But Bucky was once again thwarted by investors eager to make a fortune. Unwilling to compromise on quality, uninterested in money, Bucky abandoned the project—leaving yet another failed company.

He returned to geometry. Developing the Dymaxion map, he'd begun thinking about spheres again. As before, he thought about spheres dynamically, but now he considered them in terms of geodesics: the sailing routes taken by ships, straight lines inscribed on a spherical surface. Geodesics were the most efficient paths of travel. Bucky wondered whether a geodesic mesh—a network of travel routes realized in metal—would make an efficient structure.

His handheld models were impressively durable. The strength of the whole exceeded the strength of the parts, a phenomenon Bucky referred to as *synergy*. It was the epitome of doing more with less—and just the right structure for a new form of shelter.

✦

*Dome House*

BUCKMINSTER FULLER ERECTED his first geodesic dome in 1948. He was teaching architecture at Black Mountain College, and brought materials to build a prototype dwelling with students. The dome was forty-eight feet tall. It immediately fell.

That was Bucky's intent. He wanted to calculate the minimum amount of material needed for a self-supporting structure. A slight increase in the rigidity of his struts was enough to hold it up.

Working with students again, he added a skin. He made a scale model showing how his dome might be furnished as a home. Another model demonstrated a geodesically enclosed factory. He used universities as laboratories, engaging students in his R&D process and teaching them his philosophy. They learned about comprehensive research and anticipatory design. They learned to make more with less so that all of humanity could thrive on a planet with limited resources, a world he dubbed "Spaceship Earth."

Industry finally followed Bucky's lead. His first client was Ford, which commissioned him to enclose the vast atrium of their visitor center in 1953. Several years later, Bucky built the largest clearspan structure in the world—twice as big as

St. Peter's Basilica—as a maintenance facility for the Union Tank Car Company. There was no limit to the size of geodesic structures. Enlarging them only made them sturdier.

Their lightweight rigidity also made them singularly transportable: the first large-scale shelter that could be airlifted. The Pentagon commissioned geodesic shells to protect radar north of the Arctic Circle, and the Commerce Department used domes as trade pavilions. The first was flown to Afghanistan and assembled by unskilled laborers in just two days. Another went to Moscow, where it impressed Nikita Khrushchev. He opted to keep it.

Bucky built a dome wherever the United States sought influence, from India to Turkey to Japan. For the 1967 World's Fair, he engineered a three-quarter sphere taller than a twenty-story building, with motorized panels to control the internal climate. The American Pavilion attracted more than five million visitors. He dedicated it to Anne, on their fiftieth wedding anniversary. For the rest of the world, it stood as an icon of American ingenuity.

In the two-decade span between Black Mountain and the World's Fair, Bucky also made other structures. The most important was a variation on his kindergarten experiments with peas and toothpicks: an endlessly repeating pattern of tetrahedra called an octet truss. His truss did for flat roofs what geodesics achieved for the dome. And together with inventions such as the tensegrity mast, they represented the fulfillment of the potential Bucky had foreseen in World War I, when he'd witnessed radio waves replacing copper cables. They were cases of *ephemeralization*, in which design replaced materials.

With each new engineering feat, Bucky's clout increased. He took a professorship at Southern Illinois University— where he built a plywood dome for his family—but he was seldom in state. Traveling the world, he ran seminars and lectured to the masses. His practical approach to environmentalism and peace made him a hero of the counterculture, and his domes became the standard architecture of communes. He also had the attention of world leaders, from Indira Gandhi to Lyndon Johnson. All was as he'd predicted. The world was starting to recognize the problems he'd anticipated, and to embrace the solutions he'd envisioned.

He redoubled his efforts. His new ideas were ever more ambitious, proposed with the expectation that they would take decades to achieve. He proposed to dome entire cities for a temperate climate, and suggested that new civilizations would be more efficient if built in seaborne tetrahedra. He devised a global power grid to decrease energy waste. He proposed that world resources be monitored on an enormous geodesic globe, and equitably distributed by computer, eliminating the need for governments and motivations for war. All of these concepts were interrelated for Bucky. They were natural conclusions of his 1927 epiphany. Anyone could have come up with them. The task just happened to fall upon Guinea Pig B.

The world was ready for geodesics—and some people even backed computerized government—but no one accepted Bucky's modest self-appraisal. He was given the American Institute of Architects' gold medal and a *Phi Beta Kappa* key from Harvard. He was awarded forty-seven honorary doctorates, and was appointed World Fellow in Residence by an East Coast college consortium. And several times, he was a leading contender for the Nobel Peace Prize. On February 23, 1983, Ronald Reagan awarded him the Presidential Medal of Freedom.

The White House ceremony was one of Bucky's final public appearances. Three months later, his wife slipped into a coma. While visiting her at the hospital, Bucky suffered a fatal heart attack. Still comatose, Anne died thirty-six hours later.

## III   Postmortem

FAWNING OBITUARIES EULOGIZED Buckminster Fuller. The articles enumerated his many honors. They noted that he had received twenty-six patents, had published twenty-five books, and had circled the world forty-three times as a lecturer. *The Boston Globe* observed that the 200,000 geodesic domes erected since 1948 covered more of the planet than any other form of architecture.[3]

Each of these obituaries traced Fuller's path to success by recapitulating his personal myth. There was the expulsion from Harvard, the crisis of 1927, the AIA rejection of his 4D patent, the Dymaxion car crash: a pattern of cruel failure followed by colossal vindication. The whole narrative arc was summed up in one line by *The Philadelphia Inquirer*: "He began anticipating the needs of mankind in 1927, and after three decades of being ignored, or at best being viewed as an amiable crackpot, he became, during the 1960s, a hero of American culture."

As remarkable as this story was, it's equally astounding how little scrutiny it received. From *The Saturday Evening Post* and *Fortune* in the 1940s to *The New Yorker* and *Time* in the 1960s, journalists printed the legend. The same was true of Fuller's many biographers. The only book published during Fuller's lifetime that explicitly considered his mythmaking was authored by Hugh Kenner, a devotee of geodesics who

---

3. Many of these figures varied from one newspaper to another. According to the *Philadelphia Inquirer*, there were a mere 100,000 geodesic domes in the world. The *New York Times*, on the other hand, bloated his portfolio of patents to two thousand.

happened also to be one of the world's great literary critics. In *Bucky*, Kenner neither accepted Fuller's tale nor discredited it, because he appreciated the myth in its own right. "[E]veryone knows the story of Washington and the cherry tree, or Newton and the apple, or Watt and the teakettle," Kenner wrote. "They are mythological statements; they concentrate truth."

This concentration of truth is what made Fuller's account of his life so compelling to students and journalists and biographers. In concentrated form, his ideas were as palpable as Newton's apple, and his principles could be emulated as simply as Washington's honesty. His myth made Spaceship Earth a real place. His mythical self made comprehensive anticipatory design science a plausible job—the role we now refer to as *world-changing*, taking the concept for granted even when Fuller's name goes unmentioned.

Still, there are limits to how much principle a cherry tree can nurture, and to how much science and technology can be extracted from apples and teakettles. Clearly there's far more to Washington and Newton and Watt than can be concentrated in any given truth. And while Fuller was exceptionally fast and loose with his myth—facilitating endless remixing of the truthiest bits—his myth alone is not enough to guide the hard work of world-changing here aboard Spaceship Earth.

Posthumous scholarship has vastly improved our ability to probe the Bucky Fuller legend.[4] By knowing what he fabricated, we can better appreciate the concepts he was conveying; by keeping in mind what he omitted, we can better

---

4. The Dymaxion Chronofile was acquired by Stanford in 1999, and serious scholarly work soon followed. Two of the most notable books are *Becoming Bucky Fuller* by Loretta Lorance and *New Views on R. Buckminster Fuller*, a collection edited by Hsiao-Yun Chu and Robert G. Trujillo. Both were published in 2009, more than a quarter century after Fuller's death. Even today, most people who write about Fuller in popular media persist in recapitulating his myth.

assess the limitations of his innovations. Historical context further enriches understanding. Fuller had a tendency to claim all ideas as his own, exploiting his long life span and the poor collective memory of audiences. Chronically afflicted with petty egomania, Guinea Pig B inadvertently obscured his most original thinking, which was at the level of whole systems. To recover that systematic thought and to take up comprehensive anticipatory design science today require that his real achievements be distinguished from résumé padding. While the myth is enlightening, demystification is liberating. It disentangles Fuller's ideas from his cult of personality, and emancipates them from his acolytes, who have attempted to keep his thinking under house arrest since 1983. The significance of Fuller's myth paradoxically becomes apparent through the process of demystification; the myth becomes more enlightening when it's no longer taken literally.

In Fuller's telling, every experience is essential because all knowledge is interconnected. His intellectual autobiography is the epitome of comprehensivism.[5] Fuller didn't need literally to stand by the lakeside in 1927—let alone spend the following two years in silent contemplation—for his vision of total global commitment to motivate audiences. His experiences didn't have to all converge in reality—let alone result in innovations that exceeded the sum of expectations—for his myth to evoke the power of synergy. "It's a poet's job he does, clarifying the world," Kenner wrote. In his lifetime, Fuller was poet laureate of Spaceship Earth. There has not been one since.

---

5. It can also be read as a cautionary tale of what happens when systematic thinking succumbs to apophenia.

## IV    Spaceship Earth

IN THE SUMMER of 2008, the Whitney Museum of American Art organized a Buckminster Fuller retrospective, the first major reappearance of Fuller since his death a quarter century earlier. Writing for the *New York Times*, Nicolai Ouroussoff attributed the renewed interest to nostalgia—noting that Cold War aesthetics were back in style—while lamenting that "Fuller's brand of idealism seems more distant than ever." In fact, the utopianism underlying Fuller's thinking was on the verge of resurgence, a comeback that continues to gain momentum, making Fuller more relevant with each passing year.

Some of the first murmurings were on the conference circuit. The annual TED Prize, for instance, was launched in 2005 to recognize "an extraordinary individual with a creative and bold vision to spark global change." Early recipients ranged from Bill Clinton (for improving health care in Rwanda) to Dave Eggers (for supporting public schools with educational volunteers). Other conferences, ranging from Davos to SXSW, reinforced this rhetoric of global change, as did industry-sponsored X-Prizes, offering jackpots in excess of $1 million for the development of energy-efficient cars and affordable gene sequencing. By 2011, "world-changing" was such a phenomenon—and buzzword—that *Scientific American* began to publish an annual roundup of "world-changing ideas," such as health monitoring by cell phone and burying carbon underground.

Fuller's clout has been bolstered by this outburst of twenty-first-century idealism, and his growing posthumous reputation has encouraged it: a positive feedback loop in every sense of the word. Environmentally oriented architects and designers, including Thom Mayne and Yves Béhar, have cited Fuller as an influence. In the tech industry, Fuller's name is synonymous with unbounded creativity. (Along with Albert Einstein and John Lennon, he is one of the seventeen icons featured in Apple's original *Think Different* campaign.[6]) His reputation as poet laureate of Spaceship Earth persists. However, most initiatives falling under the rubric of global change lack the truly global perspective—the comprehensiveness—of Fuller's foremost ideas, let alone his comprehensive process of ideation. If world-changing is the ambition of our age, there is much to extrapolate from Fuller's myth, and much to appropriate from his work.

Fuller explained comprehensive anticipatory design science many times and in many ways, yet his most eloquent and succinct definition of the practice was "to make the world work for one hundred percent of humanity, in the shortest possible time, through spontaneous cooperation, without ecological offense or the disadvantage of anyone."[7] Even if the majority of his inventions were as eccentrically impractical as a house on a mast, and none of them wrought the global paradise he preached, his hundred-percent ethos was prophetic—and only becomes more resonant in a society where half the world's wealth is held by the wealthiest one percent.

---

6. The seventeen men and women were effectively transformed into company mascots, emblemizing what Apple claimed to represent. To quote from the commercial's voiceover: "You can quote them, disagree with them, glorify or vilify them. About the only thing you can't do is ignore them. Because they change things. They push the human race forward. And while some may see them as the crazy ones, we see genius. Because the people who are crazy enough to think they can change the world, are the ones who do." The ad has been credited with setting Apple on course to become the iconic technology company of our era.

7. He was speaking specifically about his World Game, discussed in Chapter 6. The quote has since become a sort of mantra for the Buckminster Fuller Institute. But even in repetition, it still stands out for its iconoclastic optimism about the potential of global thinking.

Divisiveness is exacerbated by the ecological offense of climate change, which adversely impacts developing nations to a disproportionate degree—and harms other species even more catastrophically. We are in the midst of a sixth mass extinction, unequivocally caused by human activity, in which the loss of vertebrate species has grown to more than one hundred times the background rate.[8] Atmospheric carbon dioxide levels are the highest in the past 650,000 years, and the level of Arctic summer sea ice is the lowest on record. Undermining biodiversity, rising seas and extreme weather also don't bode well for *Homo sapiens*. Enough people are sufficiently alarmed to have made environmentalism mainstream. There is broad recognition that the planet needs attention, and broadening agreement that one hundred percent of humanity needs food and water security.

Now more relevant than ever before, Fuller's core anticipatory design principles—such as inquiring "how nature builds" and doing "the most with the least"—are ready for mainstream take-up, as is his habit of bridging far-flung disciplines such as environmental science and urban planning. Drawn from diverse fields and recombined with a comprehensive anticipatory mindset, technological and scientific advances achieved since Fuller's death bring new promise to his interest in learning from nature and making the most of resources. For instance, nanomaterials can now be optimized at an atomic scale, and microbiology is revealing that evolution is the grandmaster of nanoengineering. (The Saharan silver ant is a fine example, able to forage in scorching desert sunlight, protected by silvery hair that reflects near-infrared

---

8. The latest estimate, published in *Science Advances* in 2015, compares vertebrate species loss over the past century to the background extinction rate for mammals, estimated at two species per 10,000 per 100 years. This is only the sixth time in the 4.5 billion years of life on Earth that so many species are being lost so rapidly.

solar radiation while simultaneously emitting body heat in
the mid-infrared range; construction materials with equivalent surface properties can provide buildings with passive
cooling in hot climates.) Even more pertinent to realizing
Fuller's grandiose vision is the power of the World Wide
Web to collect and communicate information. Suggestively
evoked in Fuller's most audacious schemes (such as the
Geoscope and World Game) decades before its invention, the
Web can become the ultimate tool for spontaneous cooperation when reconsidered in terms of design science principles.

The time has come to release Fuller from the zany sci-fi
designs that made him notorious, and to rescue him from
the groupies who have impounded him as a cultish prophet.
Today Fuller is rightly renowned, but for the wrong reasons.
We need to rediscover the foundations of his innovation, and
to emulate his balanced use of the world's limited resources.

The chapters that follow critically examine a broad range
of Fuller's major innovations in order to discover design
principles pertinent to Spaceship Earth in 2016, and to
explore how they might be applied by the contemporary
comprehensive anticipatory design scientist. Featured inventions include the Dymaxion Car, the Wichita House, Two-
Way TV, the Geoscope, the Dome Over Manhattan, and the
World Game. Some, such as the car and house, have become
iconic. Others, such as Two-Way TV, have nearly been for-
gotten. Several of the inventions, including the Geoscope
and the World Game, were constantly being reimagined, taking myriad forms over multiple decades. And at least one,
the Dome Over Manhattan, was pure folly (though it was
based on Fuller's most practical and profitable invention, the
Geodesic Dome).

Each of these innovations is set in historical context to
show the true nature of Fuller's breakthrough—too often

mythologized beyond recognition—and then re-evaluated in terms of modern problems and opportunities. Their broader significance as exemplars of comprehensive anticipatory design science is taken up in the final section, which explores the potential and limitations of Fuller's premise, as well as providing practical guidance on how to practice comprehensive anticipatory design science in the present.[9]

The pages that follow are informed by Fuller's thinking, as embodied in his myth and the historical record, but by no means limited to his worldview. Fuller was both a genius and a crackpot—often blissfully unaware of the difference—and he was also inevitably limited by the knowledge and prejudices of his era. World-changing has no time or space for hagiography, let alone historical re-enactment. What solutions are proposed here have been inspired by Fuller yet are vigorously independent of him. They challenge his thinking and are meant to be challenged in turn.

From his experience as a sailor, Fuller saw change all around him, and always viewed himself in transition. He called himself a verb, de-emphasizing who he was in favor of what he did. Likewise, his ideas were never fixed. We emulate him best by moving beyond Bucky, each becoming a design scientist in our own right. We fulfill his promise by each becoming Guinea Pig B.

---

9. In the course of exploration, elements of Fuller's myth will return. Motifs in this chapter will repeat, variations on a theme.

# HOW TO
# MAKE THE
# WORLD
# WORK
*Six*
*Visions*

# 1

# MOBILITY
## The Dymaxion Car

## I  The Perfect Car

THE FUTURE OF transportation did not proceed according to plan. Touted as the greatest advance since the horse and buggy when it rolled out of the factory in 1933, the first car that Buckminster Fuller built burned up in a fire a decade later. A second one was shredded for scrap metal during the Korean War. As for the third of Fuller's three prototype Dymaxion vehicles, there were rumors that a Wichita Cadillac dealer acquired it in the 1950s and warehoused it as an investment. The rumors were wrong. In 1968, some Arizona State University engineering students found it parked on a local farm. Repurposed as a makeshift poultry coop, the last vestige of Fuller's futuristic transport was slowly succumbing to the corrosive effects of rain and chicken poop.

The farm belonged to a man named Theodore Mezes, who had bought the three-wheeled car for a dollar some decades earlier. The students gave him $3,000 and hauled it home, but they couldn't make it run. So they resold it to Bill Harrah, a casino mogul with a museum full of Duesenbergs and Pierce-Arrows. He had the aluminum shell refurbished and the windows painted over so that people couldn't see

the ruined interior. In Harrah's collection—later rechristened the National Automobile Museum—the Dymaxion
car cruised into automotive history.

And there it might have remained indefinitely, a restored
icon of Fuller's stillborn vision, if a former colleague
hadn't decided to conceive a new one. The colleague was
Sir Norman Foster, architect of Wembley Stadium and the
Beijing Airport. As a young man, Foster had collaborated
with Fuller on some of Fuller's final architectural projects—
mostly unrealized—and Foster wasn't shy about using
Fuller's name to add intellectual heft to his subsequent commercial success.

Money was no issue. Foster hired the British racing car
restorers Crosthwaite & Gardiner, and had the original
Dymaxion shipped on special loan to East Sussex from Reno,
Nevada. Construction took two years, more than twice the
time that Fuller required to build the original. The back axle
and V-8 engine were stripped from a Ford Tudor sedan, the
same source that Fuller had used. These were flipped upside
down on the chassis so that the back wheels powered the
car from the front end. A third wheel—controlled by steel
cables stretching from the steering wheel to a pivot at the
back of the automobile—acted as a sort of rudder. Atop the
chassis, a zeppelin-shaped body of hand-beaten aluminum
was wrapped around an ash-wood frame. To this aerodynamic shell, several attributes from the other two Dymaxion
cars were added, most prominently a long stabilizing fin.
Adapting the best qualities from Fuller's three prototypes,
Foster's Dymaxion Car No. 4 was the idealized vehicle that
Fuller never had the funding to build: the closest metal could
get to the Dymaxion legend. Or was it?

Foster has never used the Dymaxion No. 4 as practical
transportation (let alone at the 120 mile-per-hour speed

that Fuller boasted his Dymaxion could handle). The truth is that Fuller's streamlining is unwieldy in cross-winds, the rear-wheel steering is ropy even on a dry and windless day, and the system of rudder cables is sluggish and unstable. None of which would have surprised Fuller. He refused to let anyone pilot a Dymaxion without special lessons, and he injured his own family when a failed steering component caused his car to flip en route to a Harvard reunion. He may have privately been relieved when his company collapsed shortly after the third prototype was completed. "I never discussed it with daddy, but I think the accident turned him away from the car," Fuller's daughter Allegra told the design writer Jonathan Glancey in 2011. "I think he thought that if the car did this to his wife and child then maybe it wasn't the thing to do."

Foster had no such compunction. His modern Dymaxion faithfully recapitulated Fuller's unresolved design flaws, an unabashed tribute to Bucky's genius that perversely enshrined everything wrong with the original vehicles. As Foster confessed to the New York Times in a 2010 interview, the car is "so visually seductive that you want to own it, to have the voluptuous physicality of it in your garage." In fact, the sheer stylishness of the thing was so mesmerizing that even Fuller himself lost sight of the ideas that made it truly revolutionary—far more than a futuristic mode of transport. Before the Dymaxion car became the Dymaxion car, it was a machine designed to mobilize society, rocketing people away from virtually every assumption about life in the twentieth century.

Mezes's chickens had the right instinct. The iconic object must be destroyed for the Dymaxion vision to be restored.

## II  Torpedos and Zeppelins

IN 1932, BUCKMINSTER Fuller made a simple drawing comparing a standard car body to a horse and buggy. His picture showed that both vehicles had essentially the same geometry. The hood and passenger compartment of an automobile were two rectangles roughly proportional to a horse with a tall carriage in tow. The car's grille and windshield were flatly vertical. Absolutely no consideration was given to airflow.

For the rest of his life, Fuller dwelled on this point, persistently bringing it up in public lectures and repeatedly impressing it on fawning biographers.[1] Whereas boats and airplanes were streamlined, designed for maximum efficiency, Fuller insisted that the automobile was still saddled with an equestrian past that he singlehandedly sought to overcome with his Dymaxion.

He was deceiving himself. For as long as there have been automobiles, engineers have been obsessed with wind resistance, and have been determined to diminish it with streamlining.

Racers led the way. Fuller was just four years old when Camille Jenatzy's 1899 *Jamais Contente*—essentially a four-wheel rocket with a man seated on top—became the first land vehicle to travel a mile per minute. Seven years later, Francis and Freelan Stanley more than doubled Jenatzy's record with a steam-powered car that proved *too* aerodynamic: Hitting a bump, the dirigible-inspired auto took off

---

1. "Fuller was aware that the body design of the 1932 automobile embodied only a negligible advance over that of the old horse-drawn buggies whose lumbering pace never made air resistance an attenuating factor," wrote Robert Marks in *The Dymaxion World of Buckminster Fuller*, a 1960 biography written with Fuller's close collaboration. Nearly three decades later, in 1989, Fuller disciple Lloyd Steven Sieden went even further in *Buckminster Fuller: An Appreciation*, asserting that "automobiles were still regarded as horseless carriages [in the early 1930s], and they maintained the box-like shape of carriages well into the 1940s."

and flew one hundred feet before crashing, vividly showing that the aerodynamics of flight and driving are not one and the same.

Though neither of these vehicles was practical for everyday transport, another racing car did become the prototype for most automobiles from the 1910s through the 1930s. Designed for one of the first long-distance speed contests, the 1909 Prince Henry Benz integrated the streamline form pioneered by Jenatzy into a four-seat touring car.[2] The hood and passenger compartment formed a single continuous line, a major improvement on the modular construction that automakers inherited from the coach-building trade. Looking fast even while parked, the so-called *torpedo tourer* was immensely popular and widely copied. Only the Ford Model T retained the old angularity for the sake of economy. And as streamlining became the rage in everything from buildings to fountain pens, even Henry Ford conceded defeat. To recapture his declining market, he launched the streamlined Model A in 1928.

By then, the torpedo tourer was technologically passé. As early as 1920, the Hungarian-born Zeppelin designer Paul Jaray was testing ways in which to bring concepts learned from airship research to the road. Wind tunnel tests showed that the aerodynamic ideal for a dirigible was a teardrop shape that guided airflow around the hull with minimal turbulence. Jaray flattened the teardrop to direct air over the top, ensuring that the tires of his cars remained firmly on the road.

Resembling little zeppelins on wheels (with the curved glass passenger compartment on top, rather than below), Jaray's prototypes achieved astonishing results. The standard

2. In a 1970 paper for the *Journal for the Society of Architectural Historians*, C. Edson Armi argues that the rules of the German-sponsored Prince Henry tour practically mandated that touring cars become aerodynamic. Previously, races were short, and touring competitions were strictly tests of endurance.

measure of aerodynamic efficiency is known as *coefficient of drag* (abbreviated $C_d$), with lower numbers signifying sleeker shapes. A brick has a $C_d$ of 2.1. A 1920 Model T has a $C_d$ of 0.80. A 2006 Bugatti Veyron has a $C_d$ of 0.36. Jaray achieved a $C_d$ of 0.23. Over the next decade, companies including Audi and Mercedes commissioned prototypes. Requiring complex curves beyond the capacity of conventional manufacturing, none went into production until 1934, when a Czech company called Tatra introduced the luxurious T77. Advertising billed it as "the car of the future." Several hundred were hand built, and that was the end of it.

The same year, Chrysler launched a car with a similar approach to aerodynamics, if not elegance. Touted as "the first real motor car since the invention of the automobile," the Airflow was designed in a wind tunnel by chief engineer Carl Breer, who retained Orville Wright as a consultant. The model was singularly unpopular. Approximately 11,000 Airflows sold in the first year, and a total of 53,000 were manufactured before the car was discontinued in 1937. The Airflow was just too radical for mass-appeal: Accustomed to the long hoods of torpedo tourers (which parted air like the bow of a ship), most people found the Airflow's rounded nose to be insufficiently streamlined in appearance. Breer countered that conventional cars of the period were actually most aerodynamic running in reverse, a claim supported by scientific research, but Chrysler's competition had a more effective response: In 1936, Ford introduced the Lincoln Zephyr, which integrated a more limited set of aerodynamic principles into a car that appeared swift to drivers accustomed to roadable torpedoes.

Styled by the Dutch-American car designer John Tjaarda, the sleek Zephyr easily outpaced the stubby "Airflop." Nearly 175,000 of them were built. Yet Tjaarda's impact may actually have been far greater than that. A rounded rear-engine version shown at industry events in the early 1930s might have inspired Ferdinand Porsche's aerodynamic 1932 Kleinauto—which became the best-selling car in history as the Volkswagen Beetle. Regardless of who influenced whom—and Porsche likely influenced Tjaarda in return—streamlining was well-traveled territory by the time Fuller introduced the Dymaxion in 1933.[3] Practically nobody was designing cars like buggies.

His vehicle *was* impressively aerodynamic. With a $C_d$ of 0.25, it was comparable to a twenty-first-century Toyota Prius, far superior to the Airflow ($C_d$ 0.50), the Beetle ($C_d$ 0.49), the Zephyr ($C_d$ 0.45)[4], and even the T77 ($C_d$ 0.38, later reduced to 0.33). However, Fuller was far from unique in his quest for aerodynamic perfection, and his approach was far from realistic. Compared to the Dymaxion, the Airflow was practically as conservative—and the T77 was practically as manufacturable—as a Ford Model A. The only truly unconventional car to be mass-produced in the prewar period was the Volkswagen, and that came courtesy of Adolf Hitler's central planning. Even if Detroit had decided to manufacture the Dymaxion, there is every reason to believe it would have failed in the marketplace,[5] or would have been so thoroughly compromised that people would have been better off driving a Zephyr.

---

3. The debate over who influenced whom has been going on for practically as long as these cars have been on the road. "Well, sometimes I looked over his shoulder and sometimes he looked over mine," Ferdinand Porsche said of Hans Ledwinka, the designer who transformed Jaray's aerodynamic ideas into the Tatra. It could be the motto of the whole industry.

4. The Zephyr was aerodynamically superior to the Airflow despite all the styling compromises, and despite the fact that Tjaarda designed it using "guessamatics," unaided by a wind tunnel. In the 1930s, the science of aerodynamics was still far from scientific.

5. The industry seems to have realized it, too. Licensing negotiations with General Motors, Ford, Pierce-Arrow, Curtis-Wright, and Cord all fell through.

## III    A Roadable Boxfish

NO CAR ON the street is as aerodynamic as a boxfish in a coral reef. Ungainly in appearance, with a body that looks like a psychedelic minivan, the boxfish has a $C_d$ of 0.06, just 0.02 greater than the drag coefficient of a perfect streamline.

Mercedes-Benz engineers knew none of this when they visited the ichthyology department of Stuttgart's State Natural History Museum in 1996. They were seeking a natural model on which to base a new car design, and were keen to observe the sleek shapes of dolphins and sharks. Staff scientists suggested that they look at the boxfish instead. Though dolphins and sharks have less drag, their slender bodies are not exactly roomy, and the open sea bears little resemblance to a congested city. More appropriately proportioned for a passenger vehicle, the boxfish is also remarkably maneuverable, propelling itself through crowded corals with minimal effort: The creature can swim six body lengths per second, stabilized by vortices that allow it to turn with a slight twitch of the fin.

Over the following decade, Mercedes developed a concept car with the boxfish's boxy contours. Most every alteration for the road added drag, evincing how spectacularly well the boxfish is adapted to its niche. Nevertheless, a four-passenger Mercedes prototype achieved a $C_d$ of 0.19, and fuel efficiency of 70 miles per gallon, some of the best figures on record. Presenting the "Bionic Car" at the 2005 DaimlerChrysler Innovation Symposium, Mercedes head of research Thomas Weber dubbed it "a complete transfer from nature to technology."

The process is commonly known as *biomimesis* or *biomimicry*, and it isn't exclusive to boxfish or Mercedes. In recent years, the nose cones of Japanese bullet trains have been peaked like kingfisher beaks, and buildings in Zimbabwe have been ventilated like termite mounds. For Buckminster Fuller, the inventive genius of nature was self-evident, as was the applicability of natural solutions to man-made problems.[6] His logo for the Dymaxion car was a flying fish—a chimera prominently displayed on his factory workers' uniforms— because the vehicle design was partially inspired by both fish and birds. "I saw nature used an enormous amount of pre- ferred direction streamlining," he explained in his epic 1975 lecture, *Everything I Know*. Fish and birds were shaped for efficient movement, just as he sought in his Dymaxion vehi- cle. He also followed these creatures' lead in his decision to turn his car with a single back wheel. "That's the way nature does it," he said. "She doesn't have the fish with its tail out front trying to steer."

In his observation of nature, and his adaptation of natural design, Fuller was an ancestor to Thomas Weber at Mercedes and the broader field of biomimesis. Yet, as in the realm of aer- odynamics, he was really just part of a broader movement.[7] In fact, the airships that so impressed Fuller and his fellow aero- dynamicists were themselves naturally inspired: Early in the nineteenth century, the aeronautics pioneer George Cayley designed some of the first streamlined dirigibles based on the shapes of trout. Nature is "a better architect than man," he wrote in a notebook entry dated June 20, 1809.

---

6. His mechanical jellyfish was his first of many examples, inevitably all of his own creation.

7. Once again, his loyal biographers carried the party line. According to Sieden, "Through his extensive observation of Nature, Fuller came to appreciate the impeccable streamlining of birds and fish, as well as the design of those creatures which results in maximum efficiency and low resistance in motion. Because of that understanding, he was amazed to discover that designers of land vehicles had made little or no effort to adapt Nature's unmistakably successful, aerodynamic designs."

By the time Fuller dropped out of Harvard, the utility of natural forms was almost rote. As D'Arcy Wentworth Thompson summed up in his encyclopedic 1917 book *On Growth and Form*, "The naval architect learns a great part of his lesson from the streamlining of a fish; the yachtsman learns that his sails are nothing more than a great bird's wings, causing the slender hull to fly along; and the mathematical study of the streamlines of a bird, and of the principles underlying the areas and curvatures of its wings and tail, has helped to lay the very foundation of the modern science of aeronautics."

The Chrysler Airflow was conceived in this spirit. Carl Breer first came up with it in 1927, while driving from Detroit to his summer home on Lake Huron, when he mistook a formation of Army Air Corps planes for migrating geese. His error made him attentive to nature as a source of aerodynamic design, and that insight became central to the Airflow's identity: "Old mother nature has always designed her creatures for the function they are to perform," ran an ad in the February 1934 issue of *Fortune*. "She has streamlined her fastest fish ... her swiftest birds ... her fleetest animals to move on land. You have only to look at a dolphin, a gull, or a greyhound to appreciate the rightness of the tapering, flowing contour of the new Airflow Chrysler. By scientific experiment, Chrysler engineers have simply verified and adapted a natural fundamental law." Fuller couldn't have put it better with respect to his Dymaxion.

Yet no amount of hype would have compensated for the fact that biomimesis undercut the Dymaxion's functionality on the road. Breer's Airflow only notionally followed natural models. (The ad men seem to have taken greater inspiration than the engineers.) In contrast, Fuller was adamant that his car comply with the logo he had designed. He insisted on rudder steering against the better judgment of his chief engineer, the renowned yacht and plane designer Starling Burgess, and he tried to justify his decision by repeatedly showing off—fish and birds take note—how easy it was to park. Fuller failed to appreciate the vast differences between animals and cars. Most obviously, fish and birds travel through only one medium—water or air—whereas an automobile must simultaneously negotiate both air and land. A rudder is not designed for steering by traction. A fish tail isn't a wheel.[8]

The grand challenge of biomimesis is to conceptually dissect a complex organism, severing useful traits from the living system in which they evolved, and transplanting them to a system that can be engineered. George Cayley did this brilliantly with the gliders he invented, the first to support heavier-than-air human flight. Before Cayley, people sought to fly by mimicking birds literally, flapping artificial wings that failed to keep them aloft. Discerning that birds simultaneously generate both lift and thrust with their complex wing movement, Cayley isolated the forces involved. Lift could be achieved by an artificial wing's geometry—no need for motion—and thrust could be provided by a separate fan or propeller or jet engine. That was the scheme followed by the Wright Brothers at Kitty Hawk, and it still applies to modern F-16s, an extraordinary intellectual lifespan that testifies to the deftness with which Cayley extracted flight from its natural context.

Cayley's success explains why Fuller's flying fish floundered and failed. In a more subtle way, his process also helps to explain why the Bionic Car was never manufactured. The Mercedes engineers took relevant traits from a suitable

---

8. In any case, Fuller didn't really have his biology right. For instance, most birds steer primarily with their wings.

creature, and appropriately morphed them into the body of an automobile. But like Fuller, they were too literal. They ignored crucial differences between the niche of a fish and that of an automobile. The automotive industry is built on yearly changes to car models. A naturally fit body would be an economic catastrophe because it would defy the consumerist logic of annual restyling. Until the whole fiscal ecology of cars is changed—eliminating the underlying causes of planned obsolescence—bionic vehicles will be little more than biomimetic mascots in environmentally friendly marketing campaigns.

There is one aspect of the Bionic Car that has been applied industrially: The chassis geometry was inspired by how bones grow. Bones balance the opposing qualities of lightness and rigidity by adding or subtracting tissue in response to strain, dynamically finding the minimal structure necessary for functional support. This process can be simulated in Soft Kill Option (SKO) software, which determines where struts can safely be taken away. The chassis weight may be reduced by as much as 30 percent.

After experimenting with SKO on the Bionic Car, Mercedes's parent Daimler has used the software to optimize engine supports in buses, and the process has also been taken up by competitors, including General Motors. Unlike body design, the chassis is never seen by most consumers, so style plays no role. More important, SKO shares a common characteristic with Cayley's gliders and most successful examples of biomimesis: They are thoroughly denatured, analytical, and reductionist.[9]

---

9. The vast majority have been in software (e.g., artificial intelligence based on the brain's neural networks) but there have also been applications in chemistry and physics. For instance, some portable color displays are iridescent like butterfly wings.

Such qualities have little in common with the organic, out-doorsy image of biomimicry as a wellspring of green technology. In the 2005 TED Talk that made *biomimicry* a corporate buzzword, self-appointed biomimicry guru Janine Benyus summed up the field with three questions: "How does life make things? How does life make the most of things? How does life make things disappear into systems?" The mission statement for her corporate consultancy, Biomimicry 3.8, is even more explicitly environmentalist, promising "to increase respect for the natural world and create well-adapted and life-friendly products and processes." Noble as this goal may be, it's somewhat naive. (Consider the environmental impact of air-planes, not only in terms of carbon emissions but also on the populations of birds that inspired plane flight in the first place.) Extracted from its natural context, even the most "natural" technology can wreak havoc on the habitat that nurtured it.

Yet biomimicry need not be rigidly reductionist. Like nature, biomimesis can also run wild. In Fuller's development of the Dymaxion car, streamlining was just the skin, and the rudder was a vestigial tail. Buckminster Fuller's orig-inal ambition was nothing less than to invent a new type of human ecosystem.

## IV    Biomimetic Planet

IT WAS NEVER meant to be a car. At various stages, Fuller called it a "4D transportation unit," an "omnimedium plummet-ing device," and a "zoomobile." One of the earliest sketches, dating from 1927, described it as a "triangular framed auto-airplane with collapsible wings." The wings were supposed to inflate like a "child's balloon" as three "liquid air turbines" lifted the teardrop-shaped three-wheeler off the ground.

The notion of a hybrid vehicle was not completely implausible when Fuller began designing his Dymaxion. The aviator Glenn Curtiss exhibited a prototype Autoplane at the Pan-American Aeronautical Exposition in 1917, and the engineer René Tampier actually got his Avion-Automobile airborne at the 1921 Paris Air Salon. However, their technology was conventional: fixed wings powered by spinning propellers. Fuller's vision called for jet engines to provide instantaneous lift, no runway required.[10]

As so often was the case for Fuller, the requisite materials didn't yet exist. In the late 1920s there were no alloys strong enough to withstand the heat and compression of jet propulsion (let alone inflatable plastics sturdy enough to support a plane in flight). So Fuller opted to start by building "the land-taxiing phase of a wingless, twin orientable jet stilts flying device," as he explained to Hugh Kenner decades later.[11] Fuller also told Kenner that he "knew everyone would call it a car." By the early 1930s, even Fuller himself was doing so, and after his three prototypes were built, he never seriously returned to the omnimedium zoomobile concept.

Yet the thinking behind his transportation unit was groundbreaking, even more pioneering than the jet stilts themselves. Fuller was conceiving an alternate way of living. To his biographer Athena Lord, he memorably compared that life to the freedom of a wild duck.

The zoomobile was a byproduct of Fuller's earliest ideas about architecture, which were inspired by his time in the navy. The sailor "sees everything in motion," he wrote in

----

10. Fuller was biomimetically inspired by ducks. Rather than soaring like a hawk, the duck "propels the air out from under his wing," Fuller explained in *Everything I Know*. "It's a jet."

11. Since this was a standard part of Fuller's personal myth—as mentioned earlier—he had many ways of phrasing it. The account he gave Kenner is characteristic.

a 1944 article for *American Neptune*. "Sailors constantly exercise their inherent dynamic sensibilities." For Fuller, this was the natural way of life, intruded upon by landlubbers with their manmade property laws and heavy brick buildings. For a seaman, like a bird or fish, there was no earthly reason why a home ought to have a permanent fixed address. Fuller envisioned nothing less than an Air Ocean World Town, in which housing could be temporarily docked in any location, transported by Zeppelin. To achieve this, he needed the housing to be modular and self-sufficient,[12] and he required a way for people to get around without roads. Zoomobiles promised complete air-ocean mobility for a global population unconstrained by cities and even national boundaries.

In other words, Fuller was trying to facilitate a self-organizing society, much as he had observed in natural environments. Naturally inspired, his global human ecosystem would allow people to live more harmoniously with nature. Yet his utopia was not a return to some imagined primeval idyll, for he never considered humans to be like other animals. Man is "adaptive in many if not any direction," he wrote in his 1969 book, *Operating Manual for Spaceship Earth*. "Mind apprehends and comprehends the general principles governing flight and deep sea diving, and man puts on his wings or his lungs, and then takes them off when not using them. The specialist bird is greatly impeded by its wings when trying to walk. The fish cannot come out of the sea and walk upon land, for birds and fish are specialists."

To foster a human ecosystem in which self-organization would come naturally for mankind, Fuller had to extend

---

12. See Chapter 2.

human capabilities beyond what was technically possible in the 1930s. He needed new materials and techniques to fully decouple us from our primate past.

We should be grateful that he didn't pull it off. To set billions of people loose in private jets would be an ecological disaster. As Fuller later came to appreciate, there are environmental advantages to cities, where resources can easily be shared.

However, the practical flaws in Fuller's plan are trivial compared to the conceptual promise. His world, like ours, was built on political and economic hierarchies with overarching control over resources. Through their tremendous leverage, those hierarchies have profoundly altered our environment, increasingly for the worse. Nature can inspire different social structures, self-organizing and universally local. If we want to make the most of Fuller's ideas, we need to move beyond zoomobiles and aerodynamics. From flocks of wild ducks to boxfish in coral reefs, we can sample different relationships as the basis of different political and economic systems, no jet stilts required.

Even the simplest organisms can suggest alternatives to current power structures. For instance, slime molds can solve complex engineering problems without a central nervous system: Set a slime mold atop a map of the United States with dabs of food in place of cities and the organism will find an optimal way to spread itself from coast to coast, forming a feeding network closely resembling the layout of our interstate highways. Slime molds achieve this feat through distributed decision-making, in which each cell communicates only with those nearest. The creature uses a form of consensus different from anything ever attempted by a government.

Slime molds can provide a new model for democracy, a novel method of voting that could prevent political gridlock.

Imagine an Electoral College system in which there were many tiers, such as states, cities, neighborhoods, blocks, households, and individuals. Individual votes would be tallied resulting in a household consensus, households would be tallied resulting in a block consensus, blocks would be tallied resulting in a neighborhood consensus, etcetera. (Like states in the present Electoral College, households, neighborhoods, and cities with larger populations would have more votes, but all votes for a household, neighborhood, or city would be cast as a unit.[13]) Equivalent to individual cells in a slime mold colony, people would interact most with those closest to them. Their interactions would be intimate and intense, driven by a palpable sense of mutual responsibility. Real discussion would replace mass-media rhetoric. National decisions would emerge through local confluences of interest. Political gridlock is caused by the buildup of factions and the breakdown of meaningful communication. Slime molds don't have that problem. By emulating them—schematically, not biologically—we can be as fortunate.

Slime molds suggest just one opportunity. At the opposite extreme, the global cycling of chemicals such as methane, nitrogen, and carbon dioxide may provide models for more equitable distribution of wealth and a less volatile world economy.

Maintained by natural feedback loops involving all life on Earth, the methane, nitrogen, and carbon cycles optimize the use of global chemical resources. There is no waste; every substance is valuable in the right place. That's because organisms have coevolved to exploit one another's refuse. (The most

---

13. For city ordinances and officials, the highest-level tally would be neighborhoods. For federal matters—which might include legislation as well as presidential elections and the occasional Constitutional amendment—the ultimate tally would be of the fifty states.

familiar example is the exchange of oxygen and carbon dioxide between plants and animals.) Humans can likewise cycle resources through reciprocal relationships. A minor example of this—already being tested in some cities—is the installation of industrial computer servers in people's homes, where the machines can provide warmth while keeping cool. These so-called data furnaces simultaneously save the expense of heating for families and air conditioning for cloud service providers. A global online marketplace for needs could facilitate many more such exchanges, making waste into wherewithal, transforming want into wealth. The world economy is vulnerable because of vast and increasing income disparity, reinforced by constraints on exchange that must be channeled through banks, mediated by money. Resource cycling requires no such funnel, and inherently tends toward equilibrium. We might even expect to see the coevolution of supply and demand between communities, much as happens with communities of bacteria.

With the zoomobile, Fuller pioneered a form of biomimesis that is not reductionist but systemic. Once established, the system is feral, evolutionary, experimental. In contrast to Henry Ford's cars or George Cayley's flying machines, the results are unpredictable. Ultimately, it's about setting up an environment for the organic development of a different kind of society.

Fuller the sailor was never fixed in his thinking. "I did not set out to design a house that hung from a pole, or to manufacture a new type of automobile," he informed Robert Marks in *The Dymaxion World of Buckminster Fuller*. At his best, his mind was as free as a zoomobile. "I started with the Universe," he said. "I could have ended up with a pair of flying slippers."

# 2
# SHELTER
## The Wichita House

## I  Ikea Modern

IKEA IS THE world's third-largest consumer of wood. Producing nearly ten thousand different goods, the company furnishes more than 80 million households through stores in twenty-six countries and catalogues in twenty-nine languages. Half the new kitchens in Norway are made by Ikea. An estimated one in ten Europeans were conceived in an Ikea bed.

Ikea has achieved this ubiquity by meeting common domestic needs with standardized products that most families can afford, and the $50 billion company counts financial success as a sign of public service. The corporate vision of "creating a better everyday life for the many people"— which surely reads better in Swedish—is approached with messianic conviction. "It is our duty to expand," proclaims the Ikea employee-manual-cum-manifesto, quoting company founder Ingvar Kamprad. "The objective must be to encompass the total home environment."

From flat-packed coffee tables to prefabricated houses, Ikea's total home environment is designed scientifically through a combination of economics and anthropology.

Price is the starting point for a product subsequently refined through consultation with consumer focus groups. It's a powerful feedback loop, since popularity equates to economy of scale, making products more affordable, and greater affordability makes them more popular still. In a 2013 *Wall Street Journal* article, Ikea CEO Peter Agnefjäll characterized the process of designing a new kitchen as "finding ways to engineer cost out of the system," and the effectiveness of the process is proven by the results: Ikea sells a million kitchens per year for as little as $3,000 apiece. "We have such a big influence," Ikea research manager Mikael Ydholm boasted in the same *Journal* article. "We can actually, to some extent, decide what the future will be like."

To what extent? The sheer size of Ikea gives it enormous influence, yet that power comes from pandering to popular whim. Ikea design is reflexive. The company can only really decide that the future will be cheaper, and, for a company bent on expansion, that's less a decision than a foregone conclusion.

Creating a better everyday life for the many by engineering cost out of the system, Ikea is a logical endpoint of Modernist idealism: When Le Corbusier called on industry to "occupy itself with building and establish the elements of the house on a mass-production basis"—as he wrote in his 1923 treatise *Toward an Architecture*—he could have been ordering a factory-made Ikea BoKlok house outfitted with mass-produced Ikea furnishings. However, neither BoKlok nor Ikea are inevitable outcomes of Modernism. The urge to industrially improve domestic life for the multitudes—to realize Le Corbusier's fabled *machine for living*—might have taken a different path, one that dead-ended in 1948 on a 640-acre farm in Kansas.

That's where the only complete prototype of Buckminster Fuller's Dymaxion Dwelling Machine was installed by an entrepreneur named William Graham to house his wife and six children. Just two years earlier, the round aluminum home, built in a Wichita plane factory provided to Fuller by Beech Aircraft, appeared on the cover of *Fortune* magazine. Giving it a "better than even chance of upsetting the building industry," *Fortune* predicted that it was "likely to produce greater social consequences than the introduction of the automobile."[1] As Fuller's venture collapsed, and Graham picked up the pieces in a liquidation sale, *Fortune* eulogized that "what happened to Dymaxion demonstrates the unbridgeable gap that sometimes exists between an idea and its fulfillment."

Characteristically for a business magazine, *Fortune* attributed the gap to finances and management, and scholars have since shown how Fuller's obsessiveness smothered Fuller Houses, Inc.[2] But problems of personality and money were relatively trivial. The greater issue was described by the industrial designer George Nelson at a 1948 Museum of Modern Art architectural symposium. Nelson argued that the Modernist architecture of Le Corbusier and Ludwig Mies van der Rohe had far more in common with traditionalist housing than either had with Fuller's fully industrial dwellings. The gap was unbridgeable because it had to be leaped without looking back. Nelson forecast that "the effect on 'modern architecture' of structures now possible will be as

---

1. *Life* magazine was slightly less hyperbolic. "Unveiled last week was the most startling solution yet offered for the U.S. housing shortage," announced an article in the April 1, 1946, issue. "Some called it a house, others a machine.... Although its 8,000-pound weight [actually 6,000 pounds] licked the problem of national distribution, big bugaboo of other factory-made houses, one major question remained: Would people buy such a strange house?" It may have helped Fuller's fortunes at *Fortune* that he was a technical consultant for the magazine from 1938 to 1940.

2. Martin Pawley provides a detailed account of the fallout in his biography, *Buckminster Fuller*.

catastrophic as the effect of the pioneering work of the early 1900s on the production of the academies."

Of course that isn't what happened. Instead the academies defensively embraced "modern architecture" and engrained it in the next generation of architects.[3] And as architecture schools and their alumni have increasingly focused on Modernist stylistics—or the Postmodernist game of stylistic hide-and-seek—Ikea's cost engineering has become Modernism's most profound innovation, while the Wichita House has been installed as an exhibit at the Henry Ford Museum, tended by docents posing as 1940s real estate agents.

Fuller's prototype is unlike most objects at the Henry Ford, the steam engines and passenger jets parked on the timeline of human progress. Beneath the Wichita's shell of midcentury nostalgia is a provocation to vindicate George Nelson: to build the dwelling machine that twentieth-century Modernism indefatigably promised but could never quite deliver.

## II   Machines for Living

THE MODERNIST PURSUIT of the ideal home began in 1910, when twenty-seven-year-old Walter Gropius, working as an assistant in the architecture office of Peter Behrens, drafted a memorandum enumerating the basic criteria for industrialized housing. His "Programme for the Establishment of a Company for the Provision of Housing on Aesthetically Consistent Principles" was boldly addressed to the president of AEG, the German manufacturer that had engaged

---

3. "Although the design of the Dymaxion House was unusual, it was not influential," University of Pennsylvania architect Witold Rybczynski pronounced in a 1992 *New York Times* essay.

Behrens to design a turbine factory the previous year and had retained the eminent Berlin architect as an "artistic consultant"—an industrial designer *avant la lettre*. "The idea of industrialization in housing can be translated into reality by repeating individual parts in all the designs promoted by the company," Gropius wrote. "For all essential parts the best dimensions have to be decided first of all. These standard dimensions form the basis for the designs and are to be kept in future designs. Only by these means can mass sales be guaranteed." Though he didn't make the analogy, Gropius was proposing to approach housing in the way that Henry Ford had just begun to streamline automobile manufacturing. Had AEG heeded his advice, they could have made houses on an assembly line, like the cheap new Model T.

Four years later, Le Corbusier (another former Behrens employee) sketched his first plans for Maison Dom-ino, a sort of universal support for housing roughly comparable to a car chassis. Comprising horizontal slabs separated by pillars and connected by staircases, the reinforced concrete structure was completely open and perfectly modular. Walls could be suspended anywhere, and Dom-ino units could be combined to make a house of any configuration and scale. Since this self-contained support structure could be industrially fabricated, the architect could concern himself with optimizing life inside, and optimal solutions could easily be replicated *ad infinitim*. Anticipating mass-production, Le Corbusier applied for a patent, and proposed that Dom-ino could solve the housing shortage in Flanders following the catastrophic Battle of Ypres. Instead it served as a conceptual platform for a few unique homes such as the Maison Citrohan—slyly named after the Citroën automobile—his prototype machines for living.

Those machines were, according to Le Corbusier, the first rational domestic architecture, anticipating the course all modern architects must eventually take. "I look at things from the point of view of architecture, in the state of mind of the inventor of airplanes," he wrote in *Toward an Architecture*. "The lesson of the airplane is not so much in the forms created, and one must first of all learn not to see in an airplane a bird or a dragonfly, but a machine for flying; the lesson of the airplane is in the logic that governed the statement of the problem and that led to the success of its realization. When a problem is posed to our era, it inevitably finds a solution. The problem of the house has not been posed." The purpose of *Toward an Architecture* was to pose the problem, and to provide the inevitable solution: "A house is a machine for living in. Baths, sun, hot water, cold water, controlled temperature, food conservation, hygiene, beauty through proportion." For inspiration, Le Corbusier illustrated his treatise with photos of automobiles and airplanes, such as the Delage and the Caproni, exemplifying the results of problems "well-posed." All an architect need do was to follow their example. How hard could it be?

Seemingly impossible. Just as Le Corbusier couldn't translate Maison Dom-ino drawings into physical dwellings—retreating from Ypres to make French luxury homes in the rectangular Dom-ino style—he came far short of a Gianni Caproni or Louis Delage in evaluating the housing problem, and he certainly didn't engineer a solution analogous to the machine precision of a car racing down a track or a biplane looping the loop. A machine for living, in Le Corbusier's most exacting analysis, should provide "shelter against the heat, cold, rain, thieves, the inquisitive," and should be divided into "a certain number of compartments ... for moving about freely." How many? "One for cooking and one for eating. One for working, one for washing one-self, and one for sleeping. Such are the standards for the dwelling."[4]

Certainly this was a sensible alternative to bourgeois extravagance, but it hardly required the state of mind of the inventor of airplanes. Moreover, because Le Corbusier's analysis of the problem was nebulous, elaboration on the solution only convoluted it. In less than a decade, the architect veered from the lean Maison Citrohan to Charles de Beistegui's extravagant apartment and roof garden. (Featuring electrically operated windows, mobile movie screens, and shrubs that could be raised and lowered on automated platforms, the bon vivant's Paris bachelor pad was quite possibly the ultimate machine for partying.) *Adieu, bourgeoisie. Bonjour, aristocratie!* Rigging a dwelling with modern gadgetry doesn't make the house itself a modern technology any more than cockpit seating turns a horse-drawn carriage into an airplane.

Other Modernists, including Walter Gropius, also struggled to realize Le Corbusier's machines. Collaborating with Adolf Meyer—yet another former Behrens assistant—at the Bauhaus Weimar in 1923, Gropius revisited his abandoned AEG concept with a set of "building blocks out of which, depending on the number of inhabitants and their needs, different types of machines for living can be assembled." Compact and modular, the *Baukasten im Großen* were to be manufactured in assorted modern materials, including concrete, glass, and steel, all standardized to permit any structural

4. Le Corbusier supported his argument with machine-age analogies, such as that "railway cars and limousines have proven to us that a man can pass through small openings." Twenty-three years later, *Fortune* would make an almost identical point with respect to Fuller's Wichita House: "Because it is so completely radical there is no basis for comparison with the traditional dwelling—one thinks instead of plane cabins, ocean liners, the interiors of streamlined trains, *all of which have full public acceptance.*" (Italics in the original.)

arrangement. With their engineered interchangeability, they had the quality of appliances that could be configured to process the lives of inhabitants.

The Baukasten modules were even more mechanistic than Maison Dom-ino's chassis-and-coachwork building model, but, as with Dom-ino, the machine metaphor proved too good to be true: Though Baukasten served as formal inspiration for the Bauhaus masters' Weimar residences, they never became feasible at a deeper functional level.

These early failures to make a machine for living did not dampen Modernist zeal for mechanistic housing. If anything, the industrial paradigm only became more deeply enshrined. However, without a clear idea of what function the machine must serve—without a well-posed problem— the ideal became increasingly muddled. At the Bauhaus and after, Gropius increasingly focused on the process of industrialization: how housing could be made by machine. He built blocks of identical boxes for his Dessau-Törten housing development of 1927, designed copper-clad prefabs in the 1930s, and co-developed a rapid-assembly "packaged house system" in the 1940s. His Bauhaus successor, Hannes Meyer, was dedicated to machine-like functionalism, determining the layout of housing and even their color schemes based on psychological data enlisted to make workers more productive: the house as machine for manufacturing robots. The final Bauhaus director, Ludwig Mies van der Rohe (yet another former Peter Behrens assistant), appreciated machine-age materials for their aesthetic qualities, and the formal freedom they afforded. From the Tugendhat House of 1928–1930 to the Farnsworth House of 1951, his minimalist compositions in glass and steel set the standard for elegance, forging a sort of industrial sublime: the International Style.

All of these possibilities—structural, functional, and aesthetic—are consistent with *Toward an Architecture*. The abyss between Le Corbusier's insistence on "controlled temperature" and "beauty through proportion" is so wide that architects as diverse as Gropius, Meyer, and Mies all fall in between, whether or not they were working under Le Corbusier's influence. Furthermore, mobile homes in rural trailer parks could legitimately be called machines for living, as could the little boxes of suburban Levittown.[5]

The sheer diversity of these dwellings paradoxically reveals their similarity. And if all of these are machines for living, is it really justifiable to exclude the old Southwestern adobe, the traditional Japanese *kominka*, the ancient Roman villa? Each was temperature controlled, and all achieved beauty through proportion.

Compare Corb's mythic machine for living to the machine for flying: Before the Wright Brothers took off over Kitty Hawk, there simply were no airplanes.[6] Then, in 1946, something happened. The media started calling Wichita the Kitty Hawk of housing.

## III   The Wichita House

BUCKMINSTER FULLER FIRST read *Toward an Architecture* on January 30, 1928, just months after the book was published in English. Noting in his diary that he studied it "until very late

---

5. Likewise, later designer prefabs and trophy mansions of starchitects such as Richard Meier and Daniel Liebeskind—and of course the Ikea BoKlok.

6. As with most firsts, the Wright Brothers' claim to primacy is debatable, but that isn't the issue. What matters is that airplanes were invented, whereas housing emerged out of prehistory. Even the Neanderthal rock shelter of Riparo Bombrini shows basic spatial organization that Le Corbusier's 1923 schema would classify as modern.

at night," and that he read it again in February, he identified deeply with Le Corbusier's ideas, so much so that he recommended the book to his sister with the uneasy note that he was "nearly stunned . . . by the almost identical phraseology of [Le Corbusier's] telegraphic style of notation with notations of my own set down completely from my own intuitive searching and reasoning and unaware even of the existence of such a man as Corbusier."

Fuller's intuitive searching and reasoning had begun several months earlier, when he was ousted from the construction company founded with his father-in-law in 1923.[7] Stockade Building Systems produced lightweight wood-fiber blocks used to build walls. That was Fuller's only real exposure to architecture, and it was a world apart from European Modernism: His father-in-law was an architectural traditionalist, and Fuller's own unique contribution to Stockade— beyond sales and marketing—was to develop a brick-molding system.[8] Fuller appreciated that industry might transform housing when he encountered Le Corbusier's treatise, as his letter to his sister suggests, but it was Le Corbusier's exhortation to "close our eyes to what exists"—and to reconceive housing as a machine—that set Fuller into action.

Almost immediately he started drawing plans overflowing with architectural ambition. Some he predated to 1927, ever anxious to establish his originality.[9] All are alive with the urgency of a man determined to pose the problem of housing

---

7. Fuller was forced out by stockholders. The circumstances of his dismissal are fully and meticulously described in Loretta Lorance's *Becoming Bucky Fuller*.

8. The most famous home built by Hewlett's firm, Lord, Hewlett & Hull, is the 147-room Clark Mansion at Fifth Avenue and 77th Street in Manhattan, a Beaux-Arts monstrosity that a 1911 article in *The Architectural Record* dubbed "an appropriate residence for the late P. T. Barnum."

9. By the time of the *Fortune* article, he was attributing the whole development of his house to 1927. In later accounts, he sometimes nudged the date back to 1922.

with engineering precision—and to solve it by inventing a literal machine for living.

By Fuller's reckoning, the underlying problem of the house was mobility. Like an automobile, he believed, the ideal machine for living should be mass-produced in the controlled conditions of a factory.[10] Unlike cars, he realized, there was no way to move finished houses off the factory floor. As a result, mass-production was limited to parts, the approach favored by the Bauhaus.[11] However, if houses were designed to be airlifted by Zeppelin, then they could be delivered absolutely anywhere in their entirety: They could be as self-contained and quality-controlled as the new Ford Model A. In order to be airlifted, houses would have to be light, constructed with as little material as possible. The strongest materials by weight were metals, and metals were strongest in tension. (By Fuller's calculations, the tensile strength of steel was twelve times the strength under compression.) So the optimal factory-built house wouldn't rest on the ground. It would be suspended from a mast.[12]

Sketches from early 1928 show Zeppelins dropping bombs and lowering fully furnished ten-story buildings into the craters they made. (A handwritten annotation

---

10. The Dymaxion car was a natural extension of the Dymaxion House in more ways than one.

11. Fuller was fully aware of Bauhaus developments, following the work of Gropius and Mies, along with most other major developments in architecture—and records of his scrupulous research are preserved in his Dymaxion Chronofile—though characteristically he denied any connection. In his 1955 essay "Influences On My Work," he writes that "Many people have asked if the Bauhaus ideas and techniques have had any formative influence on my work. I must answer vigorously that they have not."

12. Fuller wasn't the only one thinking about architecture hung on a mast. At almost exactly the same time, the German brothers Heinz and Bodo Rasch were working on their hypothetical Suspension Houses Project, drawing skyscrapers stabilized with cables. However, unlike the work of Gropius and Mies, this was well outside the mainstream, and most certainly would have been unknown to Fuller.

helpfully explains that cables would stabilize the towers while the craters were filled with concrete "like setting [a] big gun in war time.") Drawn in a naive style befitting their architectural oddity, the skewered cylindrical high-rises are shown in locations ranging from the North Pole to the Sahara.

A more grounded version of Fuller's idea was professionally drafted for the patent he filed in the spring of the same year. The patent application shows a conventional rectangular house pierced by a "utility chassis" that holds the house aloft and provides all the plumbing. By the time the paperwork was done, Fuller had reconceived his home as a hexagon, which permitted much simpler suspension, and he'd started thinking more comprehensively about what a dwelling machine could accomplish. The patent application was abandoned, and Fuller went public with his invention at the May 1928 meeting of the American Institute of Architects.

They essentially ignored him. (It didn't help that the annual convention opened with a statement against "peas-of-a-pod" prefabrication.)[13] So he expanded his campaign. He sent mimeographed copies of his industrial housing manifesto, *4D Time Lock*, to everyone from his mother to Albert Einstein. He also started lecturing and showing models of

---

13. Obviously, none of this coincides with his personal myth. Fuller preferred to believe that the resolution was specifically directed at him, an account of events he repeated so often, and deemed so important, that a version was included in his *New York Times* obituary. "In May 1928 Mr. Fuller offered to assign full proprietary rights to his patents covering the Dymaxion house to the American Institute of Architects. The institute rejected the offer, and at its annual meeting in 1929 it passed a resolution damning all prefabricated building concepts: 'Be it resolved that the A.I.A. establish itself on record as inherently opposed to any peas-in-a-pod-like reproducible designs.' Mr. Fuller no doubt recalled that rebuff with some bemusement when, in 1970, the institute presented him its gold medal for his contributions to architecture." (Among other falsehoods, there never were any patents to give.)

his house—rechristened the Dymaxion—everywhere from Marshall Field's department store to Romany Marie's Tavern.[14]

Bearing this mechanistic new name, Fuller's conception of the dwelling machine soon surpassed anything Le Corbusier or Gropius would recognize as architecture. His vision was truly all-encompassing. Corb had written about "a machine for living in." Fuller effectively dropped the final preposition, making the machine for living as integral to the inhabitant as a cytoskeleton is for an amoeba.

Fuller's most fully documented presentation of the Dymaxion House was at the New York Architectural League on July 9, 1929, where a stenographer transcribed his entire lecture. "Trying to find out what was wrong with the world and what I individually could do about it," he told the gathered architects, "I have come upon the thought that housing was responsible for practically all of our ills—this preconceived idea of doing things on a vanity basis rather than having things done on the basis of the clearest, most intelligent research test of science." In his judgment, solving the problem of the house amounted to scientifically re-engineering society.

The suspension system was no longer just a means of decreasing material usage and making cheap mass-produced shelter available to everyone everywhere. According to Fuller, the structure would allow inhabitants to "overcome all the elements." The height of the house would prevent flooding, the triangulation of suspension cables would protect against earthquakes, and the octagonal symmetry would streamline the casein plastic shell so that it could withstand a tornado.

---

14. The rechristening is attributed to the ad man Waldo Warren, who, Fuller claimed, also coined the word "radio." Standard etymological sources don't credit Warren, so it's entirely possible that Fuller made up the story in order to add luster to *Dymaxion* as a word and idea. In another life, Fuller could easily have been an ad man himself.

Streamlining would also optimize the internal climate. Floor and roof vents would eliminate drafts caused by air turbulence, facilitating efficient heating in winter, providing natural air conditioning in summer, and vacuuming away dust throughout the year.[15] Temperate and clean, the Dymaxion would bolster physical health, while mental health would be ensured by "drudge-proofing" the home with automated appliances to replace manual labor—including an instantaneous dishwasher—freeing people to improve themselves by reading under artificial daylight or watching broadcast lectures on television.[16] And the energy bill to keep all this technology running? No problem. Fuel would be derived from human excrement via a waste packaging toilet. In fact, the house would be entirely self-sufficient, without any need to connect to municipal sewage and plumbing. Showers would be taken with a pint of water sprayed through a "fog gun." With air delivery and an omni-transport vehicle in the driveway, people could live anywhere, and move their whole household at will. Not only would this be the end of inner-city slums' disease and crime, it would also make real estate as meaningless as the ownership of the seas beneath a ship. Here Fuller revealed his world-changing radicalism, his conception of civil engineering as a mandate to re-engineer civilization. In fact, the goal was nothing less than "to lick materialism as the basis of progress in the universe," Fuller informed the New York Architectural League. Or, as he explained it to *Time Magazine* in 1932, a house "is not a property to be owned, but a mechanical arrangement to be used."

---

15. At least one of Fuller's models included a nude female statuette lying atop a bed, Fuller's provocative way of illustrating the house's perfect climate control, which he said eliminated the need for bedclothes.

16. This was just two years after the inventor Philo T. Farnsworth transmitted the first electronic television image. CBS started to experiment with television programming in 1931, followed by NBC in 1932. Fuller would himself be involved in these early stages, as discussed in the next chapter.

According to *Time*, bankers were enthusiastic about his machine but not the economic function that Fuller considered integral to its performance. Nor did he help his cause when, asked to build a prototype for the 1933 World's Fair, he requested $100 million in funding, pointing out that Henry Ford had spent $43 million to make his Model A.[17] With perfectly solid logic, Fuller maintained that a fairground one-off was no prototype because a prototype had to model the infrastructure that would manufacture and distribute it; the housing industry was also part of Fuller's machinery.

Assembly-line logic was only part of the explanation for Fuller's untenable funding request. Fuller also had to contend with the reality that most of the necessary technologies didn't yet exist: not only televisions to edify the masses and bioreactors to convert their waste into energy, but also basic materials like durable lightweight plastics for walls and high-tension alloys to hold the houses aloft. Through lectures and articles, the machine could continue to evolve as new technologies suggested engineering solutions—and those solutions suggested additional physical and sociopolitical problems to be solved by a more advanced Dymaxion.[18]

World War II brought an end to Fuller's fantasies, and the peace that followed afforded him an irresistible opportunity. The sturdy Dymaxion Deployment Units he designed for the military—made by modifying cylindrical corrugated-steel grain bins—suggested that his dwelling machines could

17. Just as each Model A cost $500 in mass-production once the initial expenditure was made, Fuller anticipated that each of his mass-produced houses would cost just a couple thousand dollars, matching the price-per-pound of a Ford.

18. Fuller explored all of these possibilities in his short-lived architecture magazine, *Shelter*. He published provocative articles by everyone from Richard Neutra to Frank Lloyd Wright, as well as his own writing and photo essays comprising images of airplanes, radio towers, and suspension bridges—a sort of updated version of the industrial photography in Le Corbusier's *Toward an Architecture*.

likewise be fabricated from contoured sheet metal. The facilities to do so became available with the armistice, as weapons factories lost their main line of business and homecoming soldiers sought their share of the American dream. Facing a housing shortage and an idling factory workforce, most everyone agreed for the first time that traditional stick-built homes were history. Appointed by President Harry S. Truman, housing expediter Wilson Wyatt called for "widespread use of mass-production methods." And *Fortune* magazine argued that "the only way to make housing in an industrial society is to make them the way everything else is made—in factories."

That was the premise of *Fortune*'s April 1946 article featuring Fuller, illustrated with pictures of him standing on the factory floor of Beech Aircraft in Wichita.[19] Beech provided facilities and labor in exchange for an interest in his new company. It all made sense. His Wichita House channeled the logic of his prewar Dymaxion through the real-world experience of making Air Force shelters, situating his utopian vision in the context of an aircraft plant organized to produce large numbers of complex flying machines in high-strength aluminum alloys.[20] Designed to be shipped in a tube and erected in a day, the mast-hung thirty-six-foot circular aluminum dwelling was remarkably practical, while retaining remarkably many of the qualities that made Fuller housing so radical.

In terms of aerodynamics, it was more advanced than anything Fuller had previously conceived. The curvature was refined in a wind tunnel, as was the shape of the eighteen-foot ventilator capping the domed structure. This rotating

---

19. Other aircraft manufacturers, including Goodyear and Tailorcraft, were also exploring housing as a postwar product line, as was Reynolds, at the time the nation's second-largest aluminum producer.

20. *Fortune* referred to this potent combination as "the fortuitous interaction of a Puritan conscience with the atomic age."

flue aligned with the breeze. In tandem with internal convection currents, it facilitated climate control and dust removal through filters embedded in a suspended trampoline floor.

The suspension was also superior to his prewar system, balancing the house's weight with steel struts triangulated to provide structural rigidity. Walls were mere membrane, which meant they could be thin and light, and sliced through the middle with a 360-degree panoramic window. In total, the weight of the house was three tons, less than a thirtieth the weight of a conventional one-family home, and the expected price was $6,500, the cost of a Cadillac (though fifty cents cheaper per pound).

Of course much was still missing: automated housekeeping, autonomous power, television. However, the fusion of external protection and internal efficiency in an affordable, portable factory-built system put the Wichita House at approximately the same technological level as contemporaneous cars and aircraft—somewhere between a biplane and an F-14—and also plotted a direction of progress in terms of engineering. This is what separates it from the mechanistic formulae of European Modernism. Cars and airplanes are more than the sum of their prefabricated parts, and certainly more than their external appearance. The real innovation is in the integration of technologies from multiple domains to augment functionality in manifold dimensions: speed, reliability, comfort, efficiency, expense, durability. Fuller always insisted that his rule of doing more with less was different from Mies's maxim that less is more, and he was correct. There was nothing minimalist about his ambitions for the Wichita House. On the contrary, the ultimate machine for living would be fantastically complex because greater complexity would augment functionality relative to weight. Materials are replaced by intelligence—and ingenuity is an infinitely renewable resource.

Or an endless excuse for procrastination. As Beech general manager John Gaty was telling the media that his plant could make 60,000 houses by 1947—and that factories nationally could roll out two million units a year—Fuller was busy stamping completed blueprints "obsolete" and thinking up new improvements. The housing shortage became less acute. The Cold War brought new business to aircraft factories. The outmoded Wichita prototypes were abandoned and taken home by William Graham. When Fuller saw what Graham had done, he disowned the project, sniping that the architectural modifications "forever grounded this aeroplane."

He had some justification in saying so. Graham set the house on a conventional foundation, eliminating the mast and rotating ventilator. He also caulked the openings designed for air circulation. As a result, the house was extremely hot in summer, even with conventional air conditioning. The shiny aluminum shell became just another counterproductive Modernist decoration.

But the total functional failure of the only Dymaxion home ever inhabited also exposes a problem that Fuller never confronted: His machines were completely inadaptable. Ever sensitive to peas-of-a-pod criticism, he claimed that future models of the Wichita House would be available in different sizes and colors, a typical diversionary tactic of engineers confronting messy human psychology.[21] There is a crucial

---

21. In his 1938 book *Nine Chains to the Moon*, Fuller famously described man as "a self-balancing, 28-jointed adapter-base biped; an electro-mechanical reduction-plant, integral with segregated stowages of special energy extracts in storage batteries, for subsequent actuation of thousands of hydraulic and pneumatic pumps, with motors attached; 62,000 miles of capillaries; millions of warning signal, railroad and conveyor systems; crushers and cranes (of which the arms are magnificent 23-jointed affairs with self-surfacing and lubricating systems, and a universally distributed telephone system needing no service for 70 years if well managed); the whole, extraordinarily complex mechanism guided with exquisite precision from a turret in which are located telescopic and microscopic self-registering and recording range finders, a spectroscope, et cetera, the turret control being closely allied with an air conditioning intake-and-exhaust, and a main fuel intake."

sense in which conventional machines are incompatible with housing, as becomes apparent when you consider that the most mechanistic dwelling is a maximum-security prison. A machine for flying must be compatible with physics, and physical laws are predictable and unchanging. People are not air molecules. For Fuller, as for Le Corbusier, the machine analogy was misleading. Eliding the tension between maximum and dynamic, a true machine for living must be as individualistic as its inhabitants.

## IV   Living Machines

A WIKIHOUSE IS not technically sophisticated. Made of plywood and pegged together with a mallet, the house can be erected in a day by the family that will live in it. No more skill is required than you'd need to assemble a piece of Ikea flat-packed furniture. But if the architecture is rudimentary, the WikiHouse infrastructure is revolutionary. All the pieces can be fabricated anywhere on a CNC machine—a sort of robotic mill—now standard equipment in most large woodshops. In other words, the WikiHouse isn't really a building, any more than Wikipedia is a book. It's data, freely shared and fully editable.

WikiHouse software encourages alteration of dwellings. Modified in Google SketchUp, 3D models of homes are automatically flattened into bundles of 2D templates that can be sent directly to a CNC machine for cutting in any rigid material. As new dwelling models get uploaded to the open-source WikiHouse library, the range of options increases, yet all permutations remain compatible since the flattening process is standardized. WikiHouse accomplishes what Walter Gropius proposed in 1910, with decision-making transferred from a corporate producer to the individual consumer.

Still, there are limits to what can be achieved through all-embracing do-it-yourself simplicity, especially given the engineering constraints of two-dimensional CNC. WikiHouses are less machines for living than survival shacks. They are simply adequate.

Additive manufacturing can considerably increase the sophistication of the house-in-the-cloud while retaining its adaptability. For example, the Italian engineer Enrico Dini has invented a machine that can print architectural-scale structures in bonded sandstone, and the contour crafting technology developed by Behrokh Khoshnevis at the University of Southern California (USC) can output any 3D file in construction-grade concrete.

Khoshnevis's architecture is printed in layers by a gantry-mounted nozzle. The gantry is motorized, guiding the nozzle back and forth across the entire floor plan, extruding cement wherever specified by a digital blueprint. Following each pass, the gantry lifts the nozzle a step and the process is repeated. By these means, a building of virtually any shape can be made at a rate of several square feet a minute. Since the process is additive, walls can be hollow, and voids can be left for plumbing and electrical conduit. "A single house or a colony of houses, each with possibly a different design, may be automatically constructed in a single run," claims Khoshnevis on USC's contour crafting web page. Additive manufacturing offers the industrial advantages of automated mass-production without the challenge of moving whole buildings (or even prefabricated components) because the factory is mobile in its own right.

And additive manufacturing isn't limited to traditional materials like stone and concrete. A British architectural consortium called Softkill Design is experimenting with housing printed in bioplastics. Befitting the new medium, their laser-sintered models bear less resemblance to houses than to fibrous exoskeletons. In 3D printing, raw materials are expensive, but complexity is free. As Softkill's Aaron Silver explained to *Dezeen* in 2013, "We created an algorithm that mimics bone growth, so that we're depositing material only where it's necessary and most structurally efficient. It's not a purely structural object; we've also tried to 'design' with it, to create our own forms."[22]

Buckminster Fuller would have referred to this as design science, and additive manufacturing would certainly have suited his goal of making Dymaxion housing available anywhere, as evoked by another term he liked to use, *repro-shelter*. But there is also a way in which additive manufacturing, combined with the standardized adaptability of WikiHousing, goes beyond Fuller's futuristic vision by industrializing customization.

How might it work? Begin with the basics. House or apartments? How many floors? Number of square feet? Location? Budget? Architectural forms populate the computer screen, generated from a library of structural algorithms. The materials are appropriate to the location, and the structures are appropriate to the materials as well as the desired parameters. Layers of insulation are added. Methods to heat and cool the machine are selected from auxiliary libraries, as are lighting and plumbing. They are automatically woven into the structure and integrated with each other to work together. A power estimate is calculated, and means of harvesting energy are selected. If sustainable sources are insufficient, appliances are modified, insulation increased, structures changed. The process is iterative. The libraries are

---

22. Softkill's structures are developed with algorithms akin to those used by Daimler for bus chassis, as discussed in the previous chapter.

collaborative and cumulative. The process is flexible. The results are personal, yet no less optimal than one-size-fits-all Dymaxion engineering. More optimal, really, since the dwelling machine is also optimized to the physiology and psychology of inhabitants.

Additive manufacturing software and hardware will need to mature before these dwellings can be built. 3D printers will need to use multiple substrates, mixing materials as they print. At that advanced stage, the printer can also become a new kind of utility chassis at the core of the dwelling machine: an appliance that fabricates the whole house around it and alters the infrastructure over time to keep the home in equilibrium with the residents.[23]

This utility chassis would also be suited to furnishing the dwelling machine, which could be considerably smaller than conventional housing: There's no reason that possessions would need to be physically stored in closets and attics if they could be additively manufactured when required, and their materials could be subsequently recycled. Nor is there any reason why they'd always have to take the same shape. If guest beds and cooking pots are just data, Ingvar Kamprad's objective "to encompass the total home environment" would be encompassed by the house itself—no need for Ikea.

And that could foster economic changes more substantial than Ikea's one-dimensional mission to "engineer cost out of the system." When Fuller asserted that the Dymaxion "is not a property to be owned, but a mechanical arrangement to be used," he was evoking the logic of the mid-century telephone business, where Bell would lease customers the

---

23. All of this should be equally achievable in an apartment building, with individualized apartments produced and serviced by a communal utility chassis.

equipment, and the value was in the service. Similarly, Fuller's mobile and replaceable repro-shelters were meant to let families plug into a neighborhood without owning the land.[24] Future repro-shelters, licensed or shared as data, might make that feasible,[25] and the digital distribution of furnishings could replace commodity-based physical ownership with on-demand borrowing.

"In architecture, form is a noun," Fuller wrote in his 1938 book *Nine Chains to the Moon*. "In industry, form is a verb." The industrial house promised by Modernism was never meant to be a fixed machine for living. To fulfill the Modernist promise, it must become a living factory.

---

24. At a far less sophisticated level, that's what trailer parks offer.
25. With considerably more quality than in a trailer park plug-in.

# 3

# EDUCATION
## Two-Way TV

## I  Everything Has to Change

ONE AUTUMN AFTERNOON in 1959, Buckminster Fuller told some students at Southern Illinois University (SIU) that the Seagram Building was too heavy. Lecturing to the design department, he explained that strength need not depend on weight because new technology could make more with less. Modernist architecture was outdated, he asserted, and so was the competitive posturing of Cold War politicians, a needless struggle he equated with his old nemesis, Malthusianism. He assured the students that there would be plenty of resources to support the growing world population—and no more cause for war—as long as they listened to him carefully and committed themselves to designing comprehensively.

Fuller wasn't just addressing the future architects and ad men of southern Illinois that afternoon. There was also a film crew in the classroom, recording the first footage for an eighty-hour-long documentary, with a five-year production schedule, comprehensively showing Fuller's comprehensive thinking. The epic project was directed by the university's design department chairman, Harold Cohen, who had recruited Fuller to the Carbondale campus as a research professor. While Cohen envisioned that the documentary would preserve Fuller's ideas after his death, Fuller himself had grander ambitions for the film. As he told the SIU administration, consulting on a new campus they were planning in 1961, he believed that classrooms would soon be superseded by "an intercontinentally networked documentaries call-up system, operative over any home two-way TV set." Schools would become obsolete, he foretold, and all the world's great ideas would be instantaneously accessible to anyone anywhere—from New Delhi to Nairobi—elucidated by the world's greatest communicators. When his eighty-hour documentary was complete, Fuller's own ideas, as explained by him, would naturally be the first to go online.

The film was never finished.[1] Yet Fuller's technocentric educational ideas endure after more than half a century. Schools are still allegedly headed toward obsolescence, and the preferred fix is still some sort of telepresence. The rhetoric of MIT computer scientist Anant Agarwal is typical of contemporary educational thought: "Everything has to change," he said in a 2013 TED Talk. "We need to go from lectures on the blackboard to online exercises, online videos. We have to go to interactive virtual laboratories and gamification. We have to go to completely online grading and peer interaction and discussion boards. Everything really has to change."

Agarwal's opinion is based on his own teaching experience. The year before his TED Talk, MIT freely offered his introductory electronics class online, uploading video of his lectures,

---

1. By most calculations, Fuller was seldom on campus more than a few times per year, spending the remainder of his time on tour. Fuller's arrangement with SIU required only that he deliver a few lectures annually and teach occasional seminars at his convenience. In return he was given an annual salary of $12,000, as well as a large office with a staff to manage his vast archives.

as well as interactive course materials and tests, for absolutely anyone to audit. More than 150,000 students from 162 countries enrolled, staggering numbers that inspired MIT to partner with Harvard on a much broader free online curriculum, with classes ranging from solid state chemistry to social justice, each taught by a star professor, all under Agarwal's management. By the time Agarwal appeared on the TED Global stage, hundreds of universities were offering Massive Open Online Courses (MOOCs), either through his nonprofit edX consortium or one of several private MOOC platforms.

MOOCs may be the ultimate fulfillment of Fuller's two-way TV in terms of technology. Yet he would have been terribly disappointed, because the technology has wrought the opposite of Fuller's comprehensivist intentions in terms of content. Most MOOCs are as narrowly traditional as the university courses they digitalize, a phenomenon driven by efficiency and reinforced by the quest for big audiences: The courses made into MOOCs tend toward core subjects and vocational training.

"Automation is with us," Fuller argued in 1961, at the campus planning meeting where he described two-way TV. Embracing efficiency in all forms—and holding that automation would liberate humanity from the need to work—he prophesied that automated education would be "concerned primarily with exploring to discover not only more about the universe and its history but about . . . how can, and may man best function in universal evolution." Looking at today's MOOCs, there are plenty of reasons to believe he was simply deluded, irrationally infatuated with technology as a form of transcendental salvation. But it's also possible that his pedagogical legacy has been ill served by contemporary technology: that the wrong educational strategies have been automated, motivated by the wrong intentions.

Fuller's educational career was long and varied. Over a period of thirty-five years, he held teaching positions everywhere from Black Mountain College to MIT and Harvard. In those ever-changing circumstances, he consistently maintained that the innate curiosity of students needed only to connect with worldly experience for them to become comprehensive thinkers, and he experimented constantly to find the optimal way to foster that connection—to have the greatest impact on the most people. The potential and perils of automation converge on this ambition: how to automate education without educating automatons.

## II    Educational Television

TELEVISION WAS STILL an experimental medium when Buckminster Fuller first appeared on the air. He was a guest of Gilbert Seldes, the cultural critic recruited by CBS in 1937 to direct the network's programming. During his half-decade tenure, Seldes sent TV cameras out to football games and down to the ocean, reckoning that audiences might enjoy seeing sports and watching tides. He also put great store in the potential for education. "Here is a blackboard for the mathematician, a laboratory for the chemist, a picture gallery for the art critic, and possibly a stage upon which the historian can reenact the events of the past," he wrote in *The Atlantic Monthly*.[2] Explaining provocative new ideas with tangible mechanical models, Fuller's dynamic lectures were perfect fodder for the future educational platform.

---

2. Titled "The 'Errors' of Television," the article was actually what motivated CBS to hire Seldes.

Yet two decades later, when CBS finally inaugurated educational programming with an early morning show called *Sunrise Semester*, the material could not have been more conventional. Partnering with New York University, the network filmed a professor of romance languages named Floyd Zulli, Jr., recapitulating his introductory comparative literature course in a TV studio staged to look like a classroom. Seated at a desk or standing at a lectern, Zulli delivered thirty-minute lectures on the novels of Stendhal and Proust in an ersatz British accent. ("It is no mere coincidence that the word *time* appears in the first and last sentence of Marcel Proust's great work, *À la Recherche du Temps Perdu*. It is no coincidence simply because by this time you are as well aware of the fact as I am that time is the leading figure in this magnificent novel. Time and memory: Those are the things that will occupy us this morning.") Despite the tediously academic tone, or perhaps because of it, approximately 120,000 viewers tuned in daily at 6:30 AM, and 177 of them paid NYU seventy-five dollars to receive course credit.[3]

Following the success of Zulli's *Comparative Literature 10* in the fall of 1957, *Sunrise Semester* became a staple at CBS, and NBC launched a rival pre-dawn program called *Continental Classroom*. The NBC show focused on science and math, beginning with a chemistry course taught by UC Berkeley professor Harvey E. White; 275,000 people tuned in, and some 250 colleges allowed students to watch for course credit provided they pass a midterm and final exam.

Five thousand students sought college credit in 1958, watching White standing in front of a studio-lit chalkboard crowded with chemical formulae. By 1961, with Harvard

---

3. Evidently Zulli became something of a matinee idol. In 1958, Al Hirschfeld drew his caricature for the women's magazine *Charm*.

professor Charles F. Mosteller teaching probability, the number of college-enrolled students reached ten thousand. Televised education "is a very substantial and largely unexplored area," Mosteller enthused to the *Harvard Crimson*, an opinion shared by White, who told *Time* that he didn't miss the interaction of a traditional classroom setting. "Actually, most questions are asked by the dumber students," he said.

Fuller developed his vision for automated education concurrently with these educational developments in network television, and he shared his views with the SIU administration when the popularity of televised lecturing was reaching its zenith.[4] In his three-and-a-half hour oration to the university's Edwardsville Campus Planning Committee— published by SIU the following year as the book *Education Automation*—he never mentioned Mosteller or Zulli or even Gilbert Seldes, but the vast number of people watching NBC and CBS must have stoked his optimism.[5] He called education nothing less than "the upcoming major world industry."

He believed that this glorious future was a natural consequence of technological progress. Advances in transportation meant that "the world is going from a Newtonian static norm to an Einsteinian all-motion norm," he said. Soon people would consider every place home, and the local political interests that supported local schools would no longer be viable. National politics was also untenable because there was no reliable way for politicians to know the will of ever-expanding constituencies. Two-way TV was initially conceived by Fuller to address the political disconnect by letting constituents respond directly to proposed policies—"a constant referendum

4. NBC canceled *Continental Classroom* in 1963, though *Sunrise Semester* lingered until 1982.
   5. ABC also had a program, called *Meet the Professor*. It was canceled the same year as *Continental Classroom*.

on democracy"—but he realized that the interactivity would also allow viewers to call up television programs on demand.[6] There could be a vast library of authoritative documentaries on myriad subjects. "Simultaneous curricula are obsolete," he decreed. Students would no longer need to see the same lecture at the same time, as they had to on NBC or at SIU, because everything there was to know would be recorded as video, available on-screen whenever someone grew curious. "There is no reason why everyone should be interested in the geography of Venezuela on the same day and hour," Fuller told the SIU planners. "However, most of us are going to be interested in the geography of Venezuela at some time." He argued that "real education"—possible only through his two-way TV— was something to which people would "discipline themselves spontaneously under the stimulus of their own tickertapes."

It was a truly comprehensive vision: Fueled by automation, the vast new industry of education would provide lifelong schooling for everyone, and their schooling would in turn prepare them to contribute to the educational industry and to automation more broadly. "Research and development are a part of the educational process itself," Fuller said at the SIU meeting. He claimed that the system he envisioned was sustainable because the efficiency of automation would always increase, providing an ever greater return on investment. In fact, the predominant form of research and development he foresaw would occur through "regenerative" consumption: People would guide the process of automated industrialization by what they chose to purchase, and they'd become better consumers,

---

6. Fuller envisioned a system that would beam optical signals back and forth between a local tower and individual television sets, proposing that the signals could be sent with "lassers." Presumably he meant *lasers*, which were brand-new technology when he delivered his lecture. (The first working model was built in 1960.) Today the vast majority of two-way data is sent by laser, albeit through fiber-optic cables.

making wiser decisions, as a result of their automated education. Like most techno-utopian visions, it was a sort of Ponzi scheme driven by self-deception. Falling for it, Fuller enlisted education to serve technology, rather than the opposite.[7]

By the time he published *Critical Path* in 1981, Fuller had replaced two-way TV with a "world-satellite-interrelayed computer" that would provide "controlled video-encyclopedia access" for all. This computer would "make it possible for any child anywhere to obtain lucidly, faithfully, and attractively presented information on any subject," he claimed, and to ensure the quality of the videos, there would be a fully streamlined production system beyond Floyd Zulli's wildest dreams. "Those who love to teach and have something valuable to teach can discipline themselves to qualify for membership on the subject-scenario-writing teams or on the video-cassette or disc production teams," Fuller explained. "Permission to serve on the world's production teams will be the greatest privilege that humanity can bestow on an individual." Though Fuller allowed that students would "be able to review the definitions and explanations of several authorities on any given subject," the technological imperative of efficiency had all but completely obliterated his original intention of inspiring comprehensivism through spontaneous curiosity and individual exploration. Following the automation of education to its industrialized extreme, Fuller presented the perfect plan for training all of society to coalesce into a high-performance machine.[8]

---

7. Apparently SIU wasn't deceived. Despite all of his suggestions to the administration—including the advice that they should get "lots of airplanes"—the Edwardsville campus was perfectly conventional.

8. Not that it would have worked. Like many techno-utopians before and since Fuller assumed that efficiency could be increased indefinitely without compromises or diminishing returns.

Fuller could have argued that this total societal efficiency, in which regenerative consumption was programmed into a world-satellite-interrelayed global population, was desirable: that universal dehumanization was the way for man to best function in universal evolution. Instead, he simply chose to ignore the authoritarian implications of his proposed educational system. "I am certain that none of the world's problems . . . have [sic] any hope of solution except through total democratic society's becoming thoroughly and comprehensively self-educated," he disingenuously proclaimed on the page facing his description of subject-scenario-writing teams.

Fuller wasn't forced to be consistent because he wasn't actually building any of the systems he was describing. In his lectures and writings, he didn't have to decide between autodidactic open-endedness and prepackaged comprehensiveness, or to consider whether comprehensive thinking could be prepackaged. He could be hazily optimistic, dreaming his way to utopia. As so often in his prognostications, he left the difficult decisions to those who would actually attempt to automate education.

## III    The 160,000-Student Classroom

"IT WAS THIS catalytic moment," Stanford computer scientist Sebastian Thrun told *Fast Company* in November 2013. "I was educating more AI students than there were AI students in all the rest of the world combined." Thrun was describing his first MOOC, an online version of his introductory artificial intelligence course, which he'd launched two years earlier with a brief post to an AI mailing list. Some 160,000 people from 195 countries signed up. His Stanford classroom capacity, in contrast, was just 200 students.

Like Anant Agarwal at MIT, Thrun saw vast potential in those numbers. Unlike Agarwal, he decided to launch a for-profit company that would produce MOOCs outside the classroom as educational products specifically designed for web viewing. He called his company Udacity.

Along with edX, Udacity is one of the three major purveyors of MOOCs. (The third, called Coursera, was founded by Thrun's Stanford colleagues Andrew Ng and Daphne Koller; Coursera splits the difference between edX and Udacity as a for-profit platform hosting MOOCs independently generated by hundreds of universities.) Given Thrun's insistence on original content professionally scripted by in-house writers, the Udacity model is probably the closest to what Fuller had in mind with his subject-scenario-writing teams and trained production crews. Yet for all their organizational differences, Udacity, Coursera, and edX are strikingly similar pedagogically. All conform to the same basic teaching parameters because all must contend with the same technological and psychological realities.

To capture and retain student attention, lectures are typically broken into many brief segments, often as short as five minutes apiece. Each segment is edited to convey a self-contained concept, followed by a short multiple-choice quiz to engage students and provide them with immediate feedback. A longer test is administered at the end of the lesson. In the sciences and math, grading is by computer. For the humanities, essays are evaluated by fellow students. Each student is responsible for grading the exams of several others, and the grades are averaged. This compromise is presented as a benefit: The process of reviewing other students' work is supposed to enhance learning in its own right.

To simulate classroom camaraderie, students can interact through dedicated social networks, and are encouraged to meet in person with others who happen to live nearby. They answer one another's questions, eliminating the need for teachers to interact directly with the masses. Sheer numbers ensure that any query will swiftly be addressed, often more than once, and search algorithms help to organize and validate answers. Professors can monitor the social networks, and also see aggregate results on quizzes and tests. They can refine future lessons based on these data.

Social networking and peer grading are possible because courses are run on a fixed schedule, with firm due dates for assignments. Each week, all ten thousand or hundred thousand students are expected to be at the same stage in the curriculum. However, what happens within that week is open: when people view the lectures, at what speed, and how often, is a personal decision. MOOCs can thereby accommodate people living in different time zones with different work and sleep patterns and different cognitive skills.

Such is the optimized product of Agarwal's epiphany and Thrun's catalytic moment. Yet even with the combined R&D resources of the Ivy League and Silicon Valley, all three MOOC platforms have faced dismal course completion rates. In most cases, only 10 percent of the students make it to the end of the semester. Often it's 5 percent or fewer. Only half of the people who enroll bother to watch a single lecture. Thrun has been especially vocal in his frustration. "My aspiration isn't to reach the 1% of the world that is self-motivating," he told *Nature* in 2013. "It's to reach the other 99%."

The poor numbers have compelled Thrun and his fellow MOOC producers to temper their ambitions. By 2014, Udacity was seeking to motivate people by focusing lessons on practical skills that would help students get better jobs, and all three platforms were experimenting with various forms of certification that explicitly connect course completion with resume enhancement. (Exams could be proctored by webcam to discourage cheating and to add credibility to the certification process.) In other words, as MOOCs have matured, they've increasingly become mechanisms for professional development, as specialized as the contemporary job market. If they fail even at this degraded level, MOOCs will likely go the way of *Continental Classroom* and *Sunrise Semester*, which were canceled as mass audiences drifted to other interests. And if MOOCs succeed by following their increasingly careerist trajectory? They will only help to narrow the prospects of mass education, reinforcing specialization as a global phenomenon.

## IV   The Guru

A BUCKMINSTER FULLER lecture could last for three or four hours. Or it might endure for five or six or more. Nobody knew when Fuller might finish, himself included, because he didn't plan in advance what he was going to say. Standing at the podium, he simply raised his hands and began with the first thought that entered his head.

He called his lectures "thinking-out-loud sessions." They were the antithesis of five-minute MOOC lessons, and a far cry from anything that would have worked in his own proposed video-encyclopedia, let alone on two-way TV. As Stewart Brand wrote in his introduction to the 1968 *Whole Earth Catalog* (which he dedicated to Fuller), Fuller's lectures had "a raga quality of rich nonlinear endless improvisation full of convergent surprises." More than any specific invention or idea, this endless improvisation elevated Fuller to cult status on college campuses in the 1960s, bringing him his global reputation as a teacher and sage.[9]

Fuller's lectures encouraged autodidactic learning by example—his own—showing the convergences that could be found through sheer curiosity about the world, and demonstrating that those convergences were worth discovering. His insights were inevitably woven into his personal myth. For instance, he'd describe the kindergarten class in which he built a tetrahedral house out of toothpicks and peas. He'd explain that he was myopic and ignorant of what housing looked like, so he'd experimentally found the simplest stable structure—a tetrahedron—an architectural unit so ideal that it must be the fundamental building block of the universe. It didn't really matter that the tetrahedron was used in architecture long before he was born, or that his cosmology had the quality of medieval metaphysics. The substance of his lectures was secondary; they were primarily inspirational. They suggested that comprehensive thinking required nothing more than a curious mind. Anyone who heard him was motivated to emulate him—at least until the buzz wore off the following morning.

But the lectures were not stand-alone products. For all the words he used—and all the terminology he invented—Fuller was skeptical of spoken and written language. "My philosophy is one which has always to be translated into inanimate artifacts," he asserted in *Education Automation*. When he actually taught at SIU or elsewhere, his lecturing was merely a prelude to the real work of making things.

Fuller's first teaching position was at Black Mountain College, a small experimental school in North Carolina that

---

9. It helped when his audiences were high, as was frequently the case in the 1960s. When available, acid was the drug of choice.

hired him in June 1948 as a "summer substitute for a legitimate architect." He arrived with an Airstream trailer full of geometric models that he'd fabricated over the previous year while exploring the structural properties of great circles and platonic solids. Carrying them into the dining hall, he introduced himself to one and all with a three-hour after-dinner thinking-out-loud session. ("Bucky whirled off into his talk," his Black Mountain colleague Elaine de Kooning later recalled, "using bobby pins, clothespins, all sorts of units from the five-and-ten-cent store to make geometric, mobile constructions, collapsing an ingeniously fashioned icosahedron by twisting it and doubling and tripling the modules down to a tetrahedron; talking about the obsolescence of the square, the cube, the numbers two and ten (throwing in a short history of ciphering and why it was punishable by death in the Dark Ages); extolling the numbers nine and three, the circle, the triangle, the tetrahedron, and the sphere; dazzling us with his complex theories of ecology, engineering and technology.") His lecture utterly seduced his audience.[10] Entranced by his ideas, most of the seventy-four students were enticed to build on his geometric studies by helping him to erect the first large-scale geodesic dome. At forty-eight feet high, it would be more than ten times larger than the biggest model in his Airstream.

Over the course of several months, the students punched holes into long strips of venetian blind, the only material he'd been able to afford. The steel slats were then laid down on a field and bolted together, but the metal was too flimsy. Elaine de Kooning dubbed Fuller's failure the "supine dome." Fuller

---

10. Faculty members in the audience that evening also included Willem de Kooning, John Cage, and Merce Cunningham. Watching Fuller in action, Cunningham was reminded of the Wizard of Oz.

swiftly recast it as a lesson (later folded into his personal myth): By starting with a structure that wasn't strong enough to stand, and then systematically reinforcing it, you could be sure that you weren't wasting materials. The class was utterly convinced. As Fuller's student Arthur Penn later said, the dome did not stand "because it was predicted to fall down."

If the students benefited from the failed experiment, Fuller did so to an even greater extent. By the following February, learning from what went wrong in North Carolina, he'd successfully erected a human-scale dome at the Pentagon, a first step toward a lucrative long-term relationship with the US government. And the Pentagon dome in turn inspired new experiments with students.

At the Chicago Institute of Design, Fuller organized an architecture class around the problem of furnishing a dome with amenities for a family of six—including working bathrooms and kitchen—that would be as portable as the dome itself. They came up with a "standard-of-living package," a complete home interior that could be folded to fit on a trailer. They built a small-scale model. He brought it back to Black Mountain, together with nine Institute of Design students, to work on a new dome in the summer of 1949. They fit his dome with a clear plastic skin. The structure became a shelter.

Other students worked on other projects with Fuller in the 1950s and 1960s. At Washington University in St. Louis, he challenged his class to develop a dome that would self-assemble, struts extended by compressed gas. (When they succeeded, he dubbed it a "Flying Seedpod," declaring that it might serve as a rocket-deployed lunar habitat.) At the University of Michigan, his class worked on a skeletal "Dynamic Dome" that repelled rain by spinning really fast. At McGill University in Montreal, he worked with students on a low-cost paperboard dome shielded against the weather with aluminum-foil sheathing. At SIU, as the United States edged toward war in Vietnam, he had his class develop bamboo domes that he said might be a "solution" to the crisis, which he blamed, as always, on the abstract talk of politicians.

None of these class assignments was an exercise. All were active research projects, confronting problems that Fuller deemed important, crucial components of a world built upon his all-encompassing philosophy. Students were motivated not only by the opportunity to work on the cutting edge of architecture and engineering, but also by the chance to practice the sort of comprehensive thinking Fuller evoked in his epic lectures. They were invited to inhabit his mind.

Fuller generally started with a concept that extended previous innovations into new domains. For instance, at North Carolina State College in 1951, he conceived the idea of building an automated cotton mill inside a geodesic dome. The shape of the dome would allow machinery to be arranged radially on platforms suspended around a central elevator. "Thus a true flow pattern, similar to the digestive, shunting, secretive and regenerative pattern of human anatomy, will digest and process the cotton," he wrote in the course description. The mill he envisioned would take far less material to build and far less energy to run than any factory in existence. The students' task, under his guidance, was to figure out how to practically carry out his vision. "Within thirty days a general assembly and primary sub-assembly set of drawings must be developed, clearly revealing the fundamental scheme and cogently demonstrating the net economic gains in pertinent industrial logistics in metals, energy, and time investments of original installation and subsequent operation," he elaborated. "It will be clear, as the problem develops, that this omni-directional, multi-dimensional spherical patterning introduces relationships and energy efficiencies that are not only novel but to be contrasted to the present 1-, 2-, and 3-dimensional geometry limitation of intermittent batch and production lines." In other words, by working out the details of a cotton mill, the students would discover for themselves the design principles that Fuller deemed universal. In carefully controlled circumstances, working under the influence of his lectures, they'd replicate his autodidactic learning process.

The degree to which his best students were able to absorb his worldview, and to adopt it as their own, is demonstrated by the number of former students who became his professional assistants or associates. (One of them, Shoji Sadao, became his closest architectural collaborator, contributing to nearly every major Fuller project over the final three decades of his career.) Less felicitously for Fuller, the origin of new ideas sometimes came into dispute as students extended his principles independently of his classroom.

The most notorious case arose at Black Mountain, when Fuller's 1948 summer student Kenneth Snelson returned in 1949 with a sculpture, *Early X-Piece*, composed of wooden slats held under tension with nylon string. Because the tension was continuous, the triangulated structure remained rigid even if crossed pairs of slats were noncontiguous. The wooden crossbars seemed to levitate. Snelson named his system "floating compression."

Fuller immediately recognized the significance of Snelson's achievement: Snelson had succeeded in completely separating compression and tension, a structural ideal that Fuller had been touting since the late 1920s when he conceived of mast-hung Dymaxion dwellings. Fuller sought to separate compression and tension because stretched wires were strong and light. Tension was an essential aspect of doing more with less, avoiding wastefully heavy buildings. In a geodesic dome, tension and compression were integrated and balanced, making domes far stronger for their weight than piles of bricks or poured concrete. Snelson's floating compression arose from the same engineering problem as the geodesic dome, but represented an entirely different solution.

Fuller seized upon it as his own. He renamed Snelson's principle *tensegrity* and used it to build new versions of the geodesic dome—working with University of Minnesota and Princeton students in 1953—eventually leading to a 1962 patent in Fuller's name. For the rest of his life, he defended floating compression as his unique invention. "For twenty-one years before meeting Kenneth Snelson, I had been ransacking the Tensegrity concepts," he wrote in a 1961 *Portfolio & Art News Annual* article.[11] And in a letter to Snelson nearly two decades later, as Snelson continued to explore the sculptural potential of floating compression, Fuller condescendingly gave his former student credit for having come up with a "special-case demonstration" of his own principle. (At least he didn't sue Snelson for patent infringement.)

Fuller's all-encompassing ego extended beyond issues of intellectual property. He also had no tolerance for dissent. Since he believed that his worldview embodied the fundamental laws of the universe, as uniquely revealed to him through his autodidactic studies, he considered any alternative viewpoint unworthy of discussion. "I am quite confident that I have discovered the coordinate system employed by nature itself," he said by way of personal introduction in

11. Fuller wrote this article in the wake of a Museum of Modern Art exhibition devoted to his work. The curator, Arthur Drexler, had included several of Snelson's sculptures in a vitrine, and credited Snelson with discovering the tensegrity principle in a wall text. Unable to change the exhibition content, Fuller attacked Snelson in print.

*Education Automation.* But what if he was mistaken? From his veneration of triangles to his belief that automation was universally beneficial, there was plenty to dispute. In the rare cases that a pupil had the cheek to question his assumptions, Fuller changed the subject.

Fuller the guru was at odds with his own educational ideals, as was Fuller the industrialist. The authoritarian megalomania that predominated his plans for education automation also undermined his performance in the lecture hall and classroom. His rigid concept of comprehensivism paradoxically made students specialists in Fullerism.[12] He was oblivious to this paradox, naively believing that if all students thought for themselves, they would think exactly as he thought. There's no reason to think that Fuller was being hypocritical when he told his former Black Mountain student Ruth Asawa that the key to education was to "create an environment so that learning can take place." But he was clearly not the right person to create that environment.

## V   Cultivating Curiosity

IN A 1965 essay on education titled *Emergent Humanity*, Buckminster Fuller characterized the autodidactic learning process as "first taking apart and then putting together." He argued that this was the way in which people "learn to coordinate spontaneously. They learn about the way Universe works." Fuller was describing the enlightened life led by children before getting "degeniused" by counterproductive

---

12. And Fuller scorned nobody more than the specialist. In *Education Automation*, for instance, he referred to specialists as "slaves to the economic system in which they happen to function".

formal education. He saw the child's room as a "learning lab" where the materials taken apart and put together could be as simple as cloth and newspaper. Today the learning lab might be more elaborate, supplemented with programmable Arduino microcontrollers and MakerBot 3D printers.

If any educational trend is spreading more rapidly than the MOOC, it's the makerspace. Unlike MOOCs, which primarily address higher education, making extends from early childhood into college and beyond.[13] Making is motivated by a sense of opportunity and feelings of apprehension, both arising from premonitions of an impending "third industrial revolution." (The first industrial revolution was driven by the steam engine, and the second arrived with the personal computer. This hypothetical new revolution involves a recombination of the two that came before, making everyone a manufacturer.)[14] Industrially threatened by developing countries such as China and India, the United States in particular has emphasized making as economically imperative if future generations are to be competitive in the global marketplace. Maker faires have been hosted by the White House, and sponsored by companies including Hewlett Packard and Autodesk. The Defense Advanced Research Projects Agency (DARPA) has spent millions of dollars funding makerspaces in US high schools.

The economic influence of government and industry—which conflate education with global competitiveness—has made making highly pragmatic, less about learning to coordinate spontaneously than about developing new products.

---

13. Of course this depends on what gets called a MOOC. For instance, the Khan Academy, which sometimes is categorized as a MOOC platform, offers video instruction in everything from counting to number theory.

14. A key aspect of this latest industrial revolution is additive manufacturing, a technology discussed in the previous chapter.

And even this pecuniary ideal has been trivialized. Students are presented with machinery and are asked to use it appropriately, rather than being creatively motivated to find the tools and materials that will realize their ideas.[15] As a result, they follow paths of least resistance. Some of the most popular projects are custom iPhone cases and garments festooned with blinking lights. (The former is well adapted to the capabilities of a low-end 3D printer, while the latter takes advantage of washable Arduino Lilypads.)[16]

However, these faults aren't inherent to making, any more than narrow-minded career enhancement is inherent to MOOCs. On the contrary, 3D printing and Internet connectivity enlarge the potential to make things and communicate ideas. If there is a lesson to be learned from the first generation of makerspaces and MOOCs, it's that more powerful technologies call for stronger human convictions to guide them. For all that Fuller preached about technology as a panacea—and a replacement for politics—he understood the need to deploy technology responsibly. Competent stewardship of Spaceship Earth was one major reason that comprehensive learning was so important to him. Making can be an extremely effective means of attaining comprehensiveness, but only if undertaken in an environment that encourages discovery. That environment might potentially be fostered by itinerant lecturers of Fuller's inspirational caliber. More realistically, given the rarity of inspirational teaching

---

15. The problem is exacerbated by the popularity of kits. With only one correct way to assemble them, they're the mechanical equivalent of multiple-choice tests.

16. The educational establishment encourages this laziness. For instance, educational consultant Gary Stager, one of the leading advocates of makerspaces in schools, published an article in the Winter 2014 issue of *Scholastic Administrator* offering the following words of inspiration: "Imagine a sweatshirt with directional signals on the back, a backpack that detects intruders, or a necklace that lights up when you approach your favorite class." By these standards of creativity, the third industrial revolution can be expected to channel the world's resources into trinkets sold on Etsy.

relative to the population in need of it, the motivating questions and context for making can be delivered by creatively re-engaging the MOOC.

At least one edX MOOC has already incorporated some hands-on experimentation. Teaching *Fundamentals of Neuroscience* in the fall of 2013, Harvard professor David Cox encouraged students to build a SpikerBox, an open source bioamplifier kit that would allow them to hear neurons firing in crickets. Though the course was otherwise conventional—and the experiments would be standard fare in any classroom—the addition of "guided interactivity" slightly tilted the balance of power from teacher to student, and the fact that the SpikerBox could readily be modified left open the possibility that unsupervised students would find their own way forward. *Fundamentals of Neuroscience* suggests how MOOCs can become platforms for cultivating curiosity.

The cultivation of curiosity is the essential educational bridge from the child's own room to the wider world of adulthood. It's what lifts native genius from toying with anything at hand to building a geodesic dome that outperforms the Seagram Building—or finding an alternately shaped solution to the problem of architectural wastefulness. Fuller's great achievement as a teacher was to ask questions demanding answers that were both specific and holistic. His great pedagogical insight was that the process of making required the focused acquisition and integration of far-flung knowledge, an intellectual synthesis of disparate phenomena that literally would or would not hold together. You can't cheat the laws of nature.

Though the White House and Hewlett Packard would like to believe that making is vocational—preparing children to succeed in a third industrial revolution—making really has nothing to do with training engineers or entrepreneurs.

Given the right conditions, it's about the intellectual development of a flesh-and-blood species living in the physical universe. That's what Fuller had in mind when he preached about comprehensive design. Education is the design of a comprehensive mind.

# 4

# PLANNING
## The Geoscope

## I  Mercator's Folly

IN 1569, THE Flemish geographer Gerardus Mercator printed
several hundred copies of a map adapted to navigation;
403 years later, a German historian named Arno Peters held
a press conference in Bonn to denounce him. In front of
some 350 reporters, Peters proclaimed that "Mercator pres-
ents a fully false picture, particularly regarding the non-
white-peopled lands." He accused Mercator of Eurocentrism
because Mercator's world map was centered on the Northern
Hemisphere and his projection grossly enlarged the size of
European countries relative to Africa. "It over-values the
white man," Peters argued, "and distorts the picture of the
world to the advantage of the colonial masters of the time."

To counteract Mercator's slight, Peters presented his own
world map, an equal-area projection of the globe showing the
equator at the center and allotting Africa and South America
their fair share of acreage by elongating them beyond recognition. His publicity campaign succeeded to a remarkable degree, especially given his utter lack of cartographic
training. With support from former West German chancellor
Willy Brandt, the map became standard for United Nations

development agencies. UNICEF alone distributed approximately 60 million copies worldwide in the 1980s, presented under the banner of *New Dimensions, Fair Conditions*. Peters was even more explicit about the polemical intentions of his project. "The new face of the earth, as expressed by this new map, forces us to review the familiar old world concept," he wrote in his 1983 book *The New Cartography*. The Peters Projection wasn't so much a new map, he claimed, as a "new global view."

And yet there was hardly anything new about it. As professional cartographers pointed out, his equal-area projection was almost identical to one proposed in 1855 by a Scottish clergyman named James Gall, and a far less distorted equal-area projection—with the shapes of Africa and South America conforming to actual coastlines, had been published by the Swiss mathematician Johann Heinrich Lambert in the 1770s.[1] The polemical content was also debatable. After the novelty dissipated, the map seemed to suggest that the only important aspect of Africa was gross landmass, not the lived experience of the people. Most colonizers would agree with that. Most locals wouldn't.

To serve Peters's goal of challenging Westerners' worldview—and the UN's mission of promoting global fairness—a different kind of map was needed. Such a map already existed, created by Buckminster Fuller. Nor was it

---

1. A projection is a mathematical system for translating points on a sphere to a flat plane. Between the time of Lambert and the 1970s, several other equal-area maps were developed, each with a different set of priorities and compromises, including Walter Behrman's cylindrical equal area projection of 1910 and John Paul Goode's homolographic projection of 1916. One of the most popular maps in Peters's era was developed by American geographer Arthur Robinson for Rand-McNally, balancing distortion of area and distortion of shape. Robinson characterized his approach as artistic—a matter of attaining visual balance—and he attacked Peters on aesthetic grounds. Peters's distended continents, he said, resembled "wet, ragged long winter underwear hung out to dry on the Arctic Circle."

obscure. *Life* Magazine published it as a color centerfold in 1943.

Fuller's world map was designed to be cut out and assembled by readers, either as a chart or a globe. That was possible because he'd developed his projection by transcribing Earth's sphere onto a cuboctahedron, a polyhedron comprising eight triangles and six squares. With a little glue, the fourteen two-dimensional polygons could be joined to make a three-dimensional object.

But it was more interesting to leave the map in pieces, mounting each of the segments onto cardstock. "The tiles can be arranged and rearranged to animate the facts of geography and clarify many of its obscurities," explained the editors of *Life*. "The layout may be centered on any world power, and it will at once suggest the geographical considerations that dictate its strategy and ambitions."

Given that the map was published in the middle of World War II, the configurations illustrated in *Life* included the German "Heartland" and "Jap Empire," but less bellicose versions soon followed. Designed to balance accurate landmass and realistic coastlines, the flexible Dymaxion World Map was a remarkably neutral platform on which almost any geographic distribution or relationship could be objectively examined—and the easy transformation into three dimensions allowed those relationships to be transposed from a flat plane into the round.

Like Arno Peters, Fuller approached the United Nations with his idea, but he didn't just want development agencies to print a bunch of paper. Beginning in the 1950s, Fuller lobbied for an automated three-dimensional version of his chart—an enormous scale-model of the planet that he dubbed a *geoscope*—to be erected atop a tower in the East River, across from the UN's New York headquarters. His purpose was nothing less than to "facilitate the swift development of all human individuals' discovery of all we know about human life on board Spaceship Earth," he wrote in his 1981 book *Critical Path* (still trying to persuade the UN General Assembly after two fruitless decades). In other words, Fuller sought global understanding through ubiquitous data visualization—years before there were the technical means to acquire and process big data.

Data are now measured in exabytes. Visualizations are now processed at gigahertz speed on the average PC. To build a geoscope as Fuller envisioned it—technically impossible in his time—is now perfectly feasible. Yet our mindset is increasingly aligned with Peters's. In newspapers, magazines, and especially online, visual information is dispensed and consumed as simplistic infographics to an ever-increasing degree.[2]

People find the simplicity of infographics seductive, a comforting respite from the deluge of data. In the name of convenience, judgment is outsourced to statisticians and designers, rather than being taken as the responsibility of each viewer.[3] As a consequence, the increased amount of data is paradoxically making more people less knowledgeable. And it's happening as the complexity of the world around us makes personal engagement more urgent.

As Fuller recognized, a new global view is not reducible to an infographic or map. It must be as multidimensional and dynamic as the planet.

---

2. From *USA Today* to *The Economist*, practically every major media outlet now resorts to infographics either as an alternative or as a supplement to text. Search for the term "infographic" on Google Trends, and you'll find the phenomenon skyrocketing over the past decade.

3. The proliferation of infographics proves this point; publications certainly aren't rushing to print more raw data, despite the growing volume. Editors know their readers well enough to realize they aren't interested in analyzing statistics for themselves.

## II   Sailing Routes and Cholera Deaths

ONE OF THE five Dymaxion map configurations illustrated in *Life* Magazine was titled "Mercator World." Pointedly correcting the continental distortions in the Mercator projection, the arrangement inadvertently revealed why those distortions were so important to Mercator, and why Mercator was so important to navigators. All Dymaxion map configurations— including "Mercator World"—are discontinuous: The polyhedron is flattened by inserting large artificial gaps in continents or oceans. Mercator's projection was ingenious because it was a square chart on which a straight line between two points corresponded to the shortest course between two ports. On any previous world map, the straightest route had to be drawn as a curve corresponding to the curvature of the earth—known as a *great circle*—and compass bearings had to be taken constantly to keep the ship on course.

The publication of Mercator's map corresponded with—and facilitated—the age of exploration. During the Renaissance, world maps were primarily philosophical, in the sense that they allowed the mind to travel. They represented the world as people understood it, complete with dragons and serpents. Mercator's map showed how to get to those places of the imagination.

But it wasn't a simple change in course. The global voyaging enabled by Mercator provided much more fodder for scholars' maps, and gradually those maps became rich enough to afford a different type of exploration. They marked the beginning of data visualization.

The earliest examples were closely tied to the natural world. In 1604, the French geographer Guillaume le Nautonier created the first world map to chart lines of geomagnetism. In 1686, the British astronomer Edmond

Halley made the first known meteorological map, showing global wind patterns. These charts were useful to sailors. (Le Nautonier's geomagnetic lines were intended to help calculate longitude, and Halley's wind patterns had obvious utility in the age of sailing.) However, they were also worthy of study by people seeking to understand natural phenomena in their own right, and the visual strategies for conveying information about magnetism and wind were gradually assimilated into fields ranging from geology to demography.

Geology came first, grounding further developments literally and figuratively, because mapping the land compelled cartographers to map what it contained. Maps showing the distribution of minerals in Saxony were published in the 1770s, followed by more abstract statistical maps charting the distribution of commodities throughout Europe in the 1780s. People first appeared in the 1790s, with disease maps documenting the spread of yellow fever on the New York waterfront, a protean attempt at epidemiology. Yet more remarkable than any of these specifics is the intellectual paradigm shift from mapping places to mapping patterns.

The scientific power of pattern mapping was effectively demonstrated by the Prussian naturalist Alexander von Humboldt in 1817. Comparing mean temperatures in fifty-eight locations globally, he drew lines that he dubbed *isotherms* on a world map. The lines were highly warped, veering northward from Canada to Scandinavia and dipping southward into Central Asia. His map showed the dramatic effect on climate of winds such as the Gulf Stream, countering the prevailing belief that climate straightforwardly conformed to longitude.[4]

---

4. Perhaps the most remarkable feat of pattern mapping was the periodic table of the elements. By organizing known elements such as aluminum and silicon in rows based on similar chemical properties, Russian chemist Dmitri Mendeleev was able successfully to predict the existence of elements not yet discovered, including gallium and germanium.

Around the same time, thematic mapping of patterns began to bolster public policy, especially in bureaucratic France, where cartographers charted everything from illiteracy to prostitution, and began using maps as tools for correlation: For instance, an 1829 chart mapping crime side by side with level of education inspired an entirely new discipline known as moral statistics.

As the term *moral statistics* suggests, there was some ambivalence as to the maps' purpose—a tension between revealing and persuading—and that ambivalence was not restricted to social science. Even one of the most iconic scientific maps of the nineteenth century, published by the British physician John Snow in 1854, isn't as straightforward as it appears. Documenting cholera deaths around a public water pump in London, the map was presented as evidence of Snow's controversial theory that cholera spreads through water contamination. Snow was correct, but the map was not his real reason for disputing the accepted idea that cholera spread through miasma. He hypothesized that cholera was waterborne because he'd seen that patients were first afflicted in the abdomen, much as they'd be affected by swallowing poison. With houses near the pump dramatically blacked out, the map merely brought attention to his theory. It was well-meaning propaganda.[5]

This freewheeling mixture of investigation and campaigning is what carried thematic mapmaking into maturity, as European governments began publishing lavish statistical atlases that colorfully showed off their resources while

5. Even at the time of publication, Snow's map drew methodological criticism, notably from cholera researcher Edmund A. Parkes, who observed in an 1855 review that there were pumps all over London. Any local outbreak would be located near a spigot, whether or not water was the carrier; the same pattern would be seen if cholera were carried by miasma.

simultaneously posing serious questions about poverty and disease.[6] Not to be outdone, the United States began to use elaborate color maps in *The Statistical Atlas of the Ninth Census*, published in 1870. Subjects included "the acquisition of territory," "public indebtedness per capita," "the proportion of the colored to the aggregate population," and, in a more romantic vein, a "map of predominating sex, showing the local excess of males or of females." Each decade, the US Census expanded on this effort, pushing thematic mapping further into the mainstream. Themed maps enhanced school curricula and popular media.

Three and a half centuries removed from Mercator's world, Buckminster Fuller grew up amidst this cartographic bonanza. As a habitual collector of statistics and a fanatic for patterns, he was bound to contribute.

## III   The Dymaxion World

BUCKMINSTER FULLER'S FIRST world map was pure polemic. Published in his mimeographed 1928 booklet *4D Time Lock*, his *One Ocean World Town Plan* showed a globe cluttered with skyscrapers of his dubious design above a caption asserting that "2,000,000,000 new homes will be required in [the] next 80 years." Drawn freehand, the globe is shown from above the equator so that the North Pole is visible, and aircraft are depicted flying over the Arctic Circle.

---

6. The graphics were often ingenious. One 1888 chart showed the effect of new transportation technologies on travel time in France by superimposing smaller and smaller images of the French national map. (Both practically and psychologically, the country shrunk as transportation accelerated.) Fuller used a similar strategy to show "the shrinking of our planet by man's increased travel and communication speeds around the globe" in 1965.

The image was central to *4D Time Lock* because it illustrated Fuller's plan to house the world in air-dropped shelters,
and showed how efficiently his skyscrapers could be delivered.[7] But as happened so often, his sales pitch persuaded
him that he'd discovered a universal phenomenon, and the
businessman bloomed into a prophet: The sky was the new
ocean, unobstructed by continents. For the first time in history, with the rise of aviation, any point on the planet could
be directly accessed from any other. Fuller evidently believed
every word he said. Over the next decade, he sought a map
to navigate that reality.

His initial solution was to place the Arctic Circle at the
center of the page, with continents radiating out all around, as
if the globe had been skinned from the North Pole. Plotting
commodities onto this map, he could make predictions about
the future of industrialization—assuming that high-volume
air freight became feasible—as he did while working as a
consultant for Phelps Dodge. But the map was more than
that for him. He believed that he also discerned previously
unseen patterns of world history.

That was the extravagant claim he made for a version published in 1940 as part of the tenth anniversary issue of *Fortune*.
His *World Energy Map* charted both human population and
the population of what he called "energy slaves"—his vivid
term for machinery that worked on humanity's behalf.[8]
(Each energy slave was not a specific machine but corresponded to the automated "energy output of one human per
year.") His map showed that 54 percent of the energy slaves
were in the United States, and an isothermal line captured
the fact that the industrial core of America was in a more

---

7. Fuller's skyscrapers are extensively discussed in Chapter 2.
8. We enslaved energy, but our dependence on energy has subsequently enslaved us.

northern climate than industrialized Europe. From these two observations, he surmised that "history has made a clockwise spiral of civilization from East to West and northward."

He might have had a valid point, but there wasn't much on his map to support it, nor was there any good reason to chart the data from an unfamiliar polar perspective, since the position of energy slaves had little to do with Arctic routes of air transport.[9] As all cartographers know, a map is only as good as its fitness for a given purpose. *But what if the map could adapt?*

The groundbreaking adaptability of the Dymaxion world map was inadvertent. Obsessed with transportation, Fuller was in the habit of tracing great circles on a globe using a hemisphere of transparent plastic that could slide over the planet in any direction: Great circles corresponded to the edge of his plastic bowl. Drawing ever more circles, he noticed that they collectively resembled the edges of a polyhedron, and surmised that a polyhedron could serve as a simplified globe. This alone was no great revelation. Albrecht Durer showed how globes could be printed as unfolded polyhedra in the sixteenth century. Fuller's insight was that the polyhedron could be unfolded in multiple ways, and each unfolding would result in a map accentuating a distinct geographic perspective (such as the German "Heartland" and "Jap Empire" worldviews illustrated in *Life*), or it could address a specific geographic question (such as the global geopolitical consequences of digging the Suez Canal). He evocatively referred to this as "peeling data off the globe."

For his system to work—and for all configurations to be equally valid—distortions had to be distributed evenly across the map, and minimized along the edges of tiles. Fuller's

---

9. Like John Snow, Fuller had a habit of claiming that his maps showed more than was actually there, often to great propagandistic effect.

solution was to push the distortions inward, so that the map is least accurate at the center of each polygon. "[B]y having uniform peripheral scale with subsidence errors distributed interiorly of the periphery by plotting on a great circle grid, distortion is less than with any form of projection heretofore known," he explained in his 1946 patent.

When he wasn't touting the map's accuracy, Fuller liked to boast that his was the only patent granted for a map in the twentieth century, an assertion he most certainly realized was false given the research involved in filing an application. In fact, one world map patented in 1913 by the American architect Bernard J. S. Cahill—which won a gold medal in the 1915 Panama-Pacific International Exposition—had a lot in common with the Dymaxion: Cahill divided the world into eight equal lobes, splayed out in the shape of a butterfly. As with Fuller's map, each lobe was true to latitude and longitude at the edges, with distortion greatest at the center. Yet the differences in sensibility were as telling as the similarities in technique.

Cahill was obsessed with his map's symmetrical aesthetics, motivated by what he perceived as the ugliness of Mercator's projection. (Publishing his butterfly map in *The Scottish Geographical Magazine* in 1909, he ranted about Mercator's cruelty to South America as if it were a personal slight: "The lower part is dragged down and thickened in appearance until the most beautiful of all the continents is deprived of much of its symmetry and elegance.") In contrast, Fuller was motivated by the functional potential of his map's movable tiles, which put much of the map's appearance out of his control.[10] Cahill's butterfly had technical advantages, such as

10. The butterfly was not the only shape that Cahill's map could take. In the 1970s, an amateur cartographer named Gene Keyes reconfigured Cahill's lobes in the form of a letter M. But interactivity was never the point with Cahill's projection, nor with Keyes's version, and the relatively small number of lobes limits the possible arrangements.

the consistency of his grid, but Fuller was the first to make cartography genuinely interactive.

Later versions of the Dymaxion world map only increased the potential for interaction by adding degrees of freedom. In 1952, Fuller replaced his fourteen-sided cuboctahedron with a twenty-sided icosahedron, in which all faces were triangular.[11] He also eliminated country names, making his map a blank slate for virtually any thematic purpose, a platform on which a designer could express a point of view about his or her data, but the designer's perspective wasn't definitive because readers could take it apart by moving around the pieces.

Over the decades that followed, most designers missed the point. For instance, when the Buckminster Fuller Institute hosted a competition "to create a new and inspiring interpretation" of the Dymaxion map in 2013, ten of the eleven finalists used precisely the same layout of tiles that Fuller published in 1952.[12] Themes ranged from global cloud cover to deforestation to ancestral migration. Centered on the Arctic Circle, the original 1952 map depicted continental temperature gradients. The arrangement made sense. But

---

11. In his icosahedral version, two of the triangles are subdivided to allow for landmasses to remain together. The subdivisions are arbitrary, but can be ignored. More problematically, Fuller decreased the consistency of his graticule, which was already inconsistent on his cuboctahedral map. (The grid is distorted differently on each side of the polyhedron, only matching up with other sides at the edges.) As a navigational tool, the Dymaxion map grew more unwieldy. But it was a fair sacrifice to make in the service of greater flexibility.

12. The eleventh covered so much of the planet with infographic-style statistics that it was impossible to read as a map. But for misunderstanding Fuller's concept, the award must go to a Dymaxion map of the moon, which perfectly preserved the standard tiling of Fuller's preferred version—including his two broken triangles—a meaningless exercise since there are no lunar continents to make contiguous. (Even worse, the map broke up meaningful lunar surface features such as craters.) According to the Buckminster Fuller Institute, these eleven charts were selected from more than three hundred submissions. If these really are the best new Dymaxion maps—and even the BFI can't see their faults— then the future of cartography belongs to Arno Peters.

for most of the themes chosen in 2013, it was meaningless. The Dymaxion map had come to suffer the same problem as Mercator's 1569 projection: It had become an icon.

And by 2013, it was no longer really optimal for anything. Just as the icosahedron was an improvement on the cuboctahedron, there were other polyhedra with even more sides that could improve on the icosahedron. With computer processing, the number of sides, and ways they could be unfolded, became practically unlimited, as the Dutch computer scientist Jarke J. van Wijk showed in a 2008 *Cartographic Journal* paper on "myriahedral" projection.

Van Wijk's myriahedra are orders of magnitude more complex that Fuller's Dymaxion. Some have as many as 81,920 sides. Equally important, the myriahedral projections can be generated and unfolded automatically by prioritizing cartographic variables, such as whether land or water is continuous. The granularity and automation of myriahedral maps enhance all of the qualities that make Fuller's projection so powerful, and the sheer number of variations prevents any one from becoming iconic like Fuller's or Mercator's (let alone the maps of Cahill and Peters). There *is* no van Wijk map, just a system for making them, ensuring that designers make conscious cartographic choices in the process of charting their data, and encouraging viewers to question the designer's interpretation by exploring myriad alternatives.

So where in the world are all the myriahedra? Designers have yet to engage them for data visualization, despite the trendiness of interactivity. The explanation is cultural, and is related to the reason that the Mercator projection is still used inappropriately. People tend to look at a map as a backdrop, assimilating new information using familiar landmarks, whether finding a sidestreet in Rome in relation to the

Coliseum or considering ancestral migrations in relation to continents.

The seamless relationship between maps and their subjects may be more widely appreciated now than in the 1950s, yet it's still a cognitive challenge to explore novel themes on mutable projections. Viewers must be motivated, drawn away from the easy enticement of vapid infographics, a radical cultural shift at a time when only the most popular memes are widely seen. Online, challenging perspectives simply vanish into the ether.

But in the physical world, they can't so easily be avoided.

## IV   A Geopolitical Planetarium

THE DYMAXION WAS more than a map. Those great circles that Fuller inscribed on his globe also suggested a new approach to the problem underlying his cartographic interest: portable shelter. A great circle is also called a geodesic, and just as different networks of geodesics correspond to different polygons, they have different physical properties when fabricated as stand-alone structures. Some are collapsible, such as the cuboctahedron. Others are incredibly strong, especially the icosahedron, which became the structural framework for the geodesic dome.[13]

Fuller's domes embodied everything he valued in architecture, from minimal use of materials to easy air delivery—not to mention a touch of Platonic mysticism. But even as they

---

13. *Geodesic dome* is nearly as vague a term as *Dymaxion*, used by Fuller as a brand name more than a formal designation. While the earliest geodesic domes were made by bending materials into intersecting great circles, later versions were made with straight spokes geometrically corresponding to chords. The domes themselves also varied greatly in terms of both appearance and function. See Chapters 2 and 5 for a broader discussion.

evolved into trade pavilions and hippie housing, their cartographic origin continued to influence how Fuller thought
of them. A dome was the planet in microcosm. Looking out
from within, your view was global, and beyond the geodesic
shell was "your private sky," as he observed in the margin of
a 1948 drawing. Much as the Dymaxion map put the world
on your table, the geodesic dome made the entire cosmos
personal.

Four years later, while teaching at Cornell University's
School of Architecture, Fuller enlisted some students to raise
a private sky in Ithaca. Their materials were wooden slats and
brass mesh. Bent into hoops, the slats were arranged as icosahedral geodesics, making an openwork sphere twenty feet in
diameter. The mesh was then cut into the shape of continents
and attached to the surface, matching their icosahedral position on the Dymaxion map. The students oriented the sphere
on an enormous tripod so that the location of Cornell was
precisely at the top of the world, and built an observation
platform inside their miniature Earth with a chin rest at the
center.

It was Fuller's first geoscope. Standing within, students
were able to experience the world spinning by observing
the changing position of constellations relative to the continents. And the view was astronomically accurate: The star
seen through any given space in the continental mesh was
the star in zenith over the corresponding location on Earth.
Essentially it was an outdoor planetarium.[14]

This planetarium could support additional layers of information. Transparent plastic "data planes" could be added to

---

14. Coincidentally, the first known geodesic structure, erected in 1926, was also a
planetarium. The building was constructed for Zeiss in the German city of Jena by the
engineer Walther Bauersfeld. Fuller seems not to have been aware of it, and to have
developed his architecture independently.

the outer surface, marked to indicate the location of minerals within the Earth's crust or wind patterns above. In a larger version, the data could be animated by lining the interior and exterior surfaces with miniature colored light bulbs. The computerized display would not be limited to geophysical conditions, but could also show population growth, energy use, or military action. The geoscope could compress activity too vast for people to see, and also too gradual, such as plate tectonics and hominid migration. "There are many motion patterns ... that cannot be seen or comprehended by the human eye and brain relay and are therefore inadequately comprehended and dealt with by the human mind," Fuller said in an oracular 1961 lecture at Southern Illinois University. The geoscope "will make possible communication of phenomena that are not at present communicable to man's conceptual understanding."

By the time he made that speech, Fuller had already drafted his preliminary architectural plans for a 200-foot geoscope, supported by cables 300 feet above the East River, astride the United Nations headquarters in midtown New York. The height was chosen so that the globe would match the height of the tallest building in the UN complex, and would be visible to any delegate looking out the window. The diameter was selected so that the whole world would be visible at once, yet details as small as an individual house could be represented on the surface. There was obviously a strong polemical bent to this plan, as politically calculated as Arno Peters's equal-area world map. "The 200-foot-size Geoscope would make it possible for humans to identify the true scale of themselves and their activities on our planet," Fuller wrote in *Critical Path*. It was the ultimate physical expression of everything he meant when he spoke of human connectedness and codependence aboard Spaceship Earth.

Yet what made the geoscope more than a magnificently expensive public monument—for which Fuller sought $10 million in UN funding—was the potential for monumental data visualization to inform communal problem-solving. Developing some of the core ideas from his Southern Illinois University lecture, he wrote in *Critical Path* that "many of today's seemingly completely new and complex occurrences are in fact relatively simple and are clearly related to other phenomena with which we have learned to deal successfully. With the Geoscope humanity would be able to recognize formerly invisible patterns and thereby to forecast and plan in vastly greater magnitude than heretofore." The geoscope would become a hub of collective intelligence.

Given the importance of this advance, Fuller didn't limit his lobbying to the United Nations. He also pitched the United States Information Agency (USIA) when the government sought his ideas for the 1967 World's Fair. He proposed a 400-foot dome containing a 100-foot icosahedral globe that would automatically unfold into a Dymaxion map. The map would be animated with a hundred thousand flickering lights, showing globally meaningful patterns that would "regain the spontaneous admiration and confidence of the whole world."[15]

Spontaneous admiration wasn't exactly what the USIA had in mind. The government commissioned Fuller's dome—a 250-foot version—but filled it with unequivocal examples of American accomplishment, such as NASA spacecraft and Raggedy Ann dolls. Fuller's cartography was included in the pavilion only incidentally: In a small Pop art exhibit, Jasper Johns depicted Fuller's Dymaxion

---

15. Fuller intended this map to be the basis for a World Game to be played by visitors to Expo 67, as discussed in Chapter 6.

map in an encaustic painting on triangular panels. Johns's *Map* replicated the strategy of his earlier paintings of the American flag: flat depictions of a symbol, painted by hand, that slyly questioned what depiction meant. The *Flag* paintings relied on the American flag as an emblem devoid of representational content. His *Map* suggested that the Dymaxion icosahedron was already becoming as purely symbolic as the Stars and Stripes.

Yet Johns was the most philosophically subtle of all the Pop artists. In his *Flag* paintings, the vigorous brushwork lures the viewer back into the realm of physicality. At the same instant the painting becomes a flag, the flag becomes a painting. This quality of profound indeterminacy is possible because the experience is visual. The brain processes visual stimuli with such alacrity that multiple meanings can coexist, overlap, and interact. Like good art, great data visualization taps into that.[16]

## V   Your Local Globe

THE HUMAN BRAIN is the most complex structure in the known universe. A hundred trillion synapses connect a hundred billion neurons, and that's only one level of complication, much as streets are just one layer of urban infrastructure. The deepest efforts to understand the brain rely on a complete map of synapses, but also depend on exploration of higher-level structures such as lobes, and more basic systems such as the ion channels that produce neural signals. Experimental

---

16. Around the same time as Johns was painting flags and maps, information visualization was coming into full maturity, most significantly through American mathematician John Tukey's development of Exploratory Data Analysis.

data at all levels are being published at a rate no individual can possibly read. If the human brain is ever to comprehend itself, it will happen through visualization techniques.

That's why neuroscientists are now producing some of the most complex visualizations in the known universe. The most sophisticated, currently undergoing development in Switzerland, is an immersive 3D environment encompassing all levels of brain structure and functionality. Researchers can look at this three-dimensional brain map at any level of detail, from molecular interactions to gross anatomy, and can also simulate mental activity. Inputs can be modulated, structures modified, and outputs measured. Patterns can be observed and tested. While the model is still rudimentary, and vastly more lab research is needed, the big data visualization of the Human Brain Project has holistic ambition befitting Buckminster Fuller. It's a geoscope of the mind.

Of course the brain is not the only beneficiary of scientific and technological advances since Fuller's death. Networks of sensors now provide a constant feed of physical and biological data about the planet, plotted onto the globe with satellite-guided precision. Human interactions are also monitored more closely than at any time in history, whether by social media or government surveillance. There's enough information for a geoscope of the planet—animated in real time, as Fuller envisioned—and far too much data to understand the world without it.

The potential is already evident in some of the data visualizations scattered across the web. Many of these are straightforward, such as WNYC's median income map of the United States extracted from census data in 2011.[17] Color-coded by income bracket, the map is zoomable from nation to

17. http://project.wnyc.org/median-income-nation

neighborhood. A similar interface works for less traditional themes, including hatred and happiness. Data on both of these has been culled from Twitter by monitoring the language of geotagged tweets. The map of hatred, produced at Humboldt State University, shows how often select epithets were derisively used over a one-year period from 2012 to 2013.[18] (*Fag* is common throughout the South and Midwest; *wetback* is confined almost entirely to Texas.) The happiness map is an ongoing University of Vermont project, updated daily, monitoring the frequency of thousands of words.[19] (*Sex* and *lol* are rated happier than *suicide* and *sucks*.) In each of these cases, as with the median income map, discovery is a function of personal exploration. Patterns emerge through interaction.

At least as compelling are maps that enlist data to reveal alternative geographies of familiar places. In 2013, a land use planner at the Sonoran Institute named John Lavey redrew state lines according to water supply, so that each state would have its own watershed and no two states would fight over the same aquifer.[20] Around the same time, a Northwestern University physicist named Dirk Brockmann showed how state lines could be redrawn according to the movement of cash—which tends to circulate in a confined area that doesn't conform to political borders—arguing that these "effective communities" were more meaningful than those mandated by the Founding Fathers.[21] Individually, these maps are provocatively interpretive. Explored in tandem, they reveal

18. http://users.humboldt.edu/mstephens/hate/hate_map.html
19. http://hedonometer.org/maps.html
20. http://communitybuilders.net/the-united-watershed-states-of-america/
21. Brockmann based his map on data collected by wheresgeorge.com, a website that tracks the whereabouts of money. Volunteers log the serial numbers on all the banknotes that pass through their hands. Circulation patterns emerge when the same serial number is logged more than once. Brockman's map can be seen here: http://rocs.hu-berlin.de/projects/borders/index.html

inadvertent overlaps, such as the ever-evolving relationship between riverways and trade.

The democratization of data sets and visualization tools—often in a single package like Google's Public Data Explorer—undoubtedly fosters cartographic creativity, but the laissez-faire freedom undermines the cumulative potential of mapping. Online dissemination through social media only exacerbates the problem since people see only what already interests them. Despite the obvious common ground—Earth itself—there is no unified cartographic initiative equivalent to the Human Brain Project.

Fuller was already warning about the consequences of fragmentation in his 1963 book *Operating Manual for Spaceship Earth,* where he noted that "society operates on the theory that specialization is the key to success, not realizing that specialization precludes comprehensive thinking." One of the underlying motivations for building a geoscope in the 1960s, the need for a unifying view, is ever more apposite.

Which is not to say that Fuller's grandiose East River plans should be revived. His privileging of New York goes against the geoscope's compellingly global premise. Moreover, what appeared to be a great technological feat in the 1980s now seems technically trivial. All that's required is a sphere large enough to support big data in sufficient detail for relationships between global and local phenomena to be perceptible: essentially a convex screen with internal projection, potentially networked with other geoscopes to share the same sensors, data processing, and computer modeling.

Any community could host one or more orbs, much as most communities host public sculpture. They could be made to different scales, located in town halls and public squares. Everyone everywhere would be able to draw on the shared computing resources to contribute visualizations—much as anyone can contribute content to the Web—but each orb would be locally curated, much like public television. The monumental presence in a public location would fully engage people's eyes and mind. Equally important, it would provide a locus for collective discovery and action.

Gerardus Mercator's world map of 1569 pictured global circumnavigation as a network of straight lines between ports, a network that has progressively increased in intricacy to an extent that every point on Earth has a direct effect on all others. All local activity is now global. The whole world subsists in every village. It just isn't yet visible.

# 5

# ENVIRONMENT
## The Dome Over Manhattan

## I  The Geoengineers

SCULTHORPE AIRFIELD WAS built in 1942 as a North Sea outpost for the Allies to battle the Axis. Seventy-one years later, some scientists from Bristol and Cambridge Universities converged on Sculthorpe to practice maneuvers against a far more elusive adversary: global climate change. They dubbed their initiative the Stratospheric Particle Injection for Climate Engineering Project, and their weapons were a weather balloon, a sidewalk pressure washer, and a kilometer of plastic hose, with which they planned to blast a vat of water into the atmosphere. The experiment would help to determine whether reflective sulfate particles could likewise be pumped into the sky to deflect sunlight, cooling the planet by reducing our exposure to solar radiation.

The balloon never got off the ground. Despite the fact that the water was as innocuous as rain, an international consortium of environmental organizations led by the ETC Group petitioned the British government to stop the launch. They objected because the exercise would have been one of the first practical experiments in geoengineering. They argued that it would legitimate the concept of commandeering the climate.[1]

Though their position was extreme, concerns about geo-engineering are shared by most climate scientists (including the researchers attempting the Sculthorpe experiment).[2] The global climate is terrifically complex. Computer models can scarcely predict the behavior of a hurricane off the coast of Florida, let alone model hundred-year feedback loops between the atmosphere, the oceans, and all life on Earth. Scientists can be pretty sure about the immediate effect of spraying the stratosphere with sulfate aerosols, since volcanoes emit sulfates that temporarily shade the planet from sunlight. (Geomimesis of a sort: that's how geoengineers got the idea in the first place.) But volcanic eruptions are intermittent; a geoengineering scheme known as solar radiation management—SRM in geoengineering jargon—would need to be maintained constantly until society substantially lowered greenhouse gas emissions and global temperatures responded to the decrease.

The process could take thousands of years.[3] Since the technology cannot be tested in advance—beyond simple feasibility studies like the Sculthorpe balloon trial—most side effects will remain unknown until they're ubiquitous. A 2013 study

---

1. As the ETC Group argued in a 2009 special report titled *The Emperor's New Climate*, "small-scale tests will forever be regarded as inadequate and pressure will come to bear to move swiftly to larger-scale interventions (with greater risk and less predictability). . . . This pattern is familiar to people who know the history of genetically modified crops and nuclear weapons."

2. University of Bristol climate scientist Matthew Watson, one of the leaders of the Stratospheric Particle Injection for Climate Engineering Project, encapsulates scientists' ambivalence toward geoengineering in the name of his blog, *The Reluctant Geoengineer*. "If we do this, it will be the clearest indication we have failed as planetary stewards," he told *The Independent* (UK) in a 2013 interview. "It will be a desperate thing to do."

3. Geoengineering could actually increase the time span by decreasing the incentive to lower carbon emissions. As the ETC Group phrases it, "the illusion of a 'techno-fix' serves as an all too convenient excuse for the powerful to drag their heels and further refrain from making the urgent changes required to reverse the climate's trajectory."

by the National Center for Atmospheric Research illustrates the irreducible complexity of the environment, revealing how solar radiation management could unexpectedly impact rainfall. Simple models showed no net change in precipitation because evaporation would simultaneously be boosted by global warming and dampened by sun shading, but those models didn't take into account the effect of carbon dioxide on plants. Leaf pores shrink in response to $CO_2$, reducing how much water vapor they release. If temperatures are sustained while $CO_2$ levels rise, rainfall could plummet. And that could have further unknown effects—if the model is even correct.

Mastering the climate at a planetary scale may never be feasible. After all, the world is not a human invention. But cities are. They're the largest human habitats. The biggest, Tokyo, has nearly 40 million residents. More than half the world's 7 billion people live in cities, escalating to an anticipated 70 percent by 2040. Given that cities occupy just 2 percent of the world's landmass, mastering their climate won't have a direct impact on global temperatures. Given that cities consume 75 percent of the world's resources, and produce nearly three-quarters of the world's greenhouse gases—one-twentieth of global electricity is consumed by air conditioning alone—mastering urban climate is a reasonable way to manage the ultimate source of climate change: energy consumption.

So, how do you control a city's climate? Why not set it under a dome?


## II    Doming over Manhattan

BUCKMINSTER FULLER MADE his first skybreak in 1949: a geodesic dome covered with a transparent plastic skin. It wasn't much to look at. In fact, when he set the structure outdoors, the thin metal struts seemed nearly to disappear. That was the principal characteristic of a skybreak: The transparent geodesic dome was shelter at its most minimalistic.

Fuller refined his concept over the next decade. He reconceived the skin as a set of transparent panels, motorized to provide inhabitants with total control of the internal climate. The skybreak would be furnished with the usual amenities—bed, bath, and kitchen—but privacy would be provided by trees instead of walls. With a full view of the sky above and foliage all around them, residents would have the sensation of living in a garden without the discomforts of cold or rain.[4]

It might have been the ultimate luxury villa—a refuge even more spectacular than Frank Lloyd Wright's *Falling Water*—but Fuller was never interested in opulence. His motivation, as always, was parsimoniousness. "The way consumption curves are going in many of our big cities it is clear that we are running out of energy," he asserted in *The Dymaxion World of Buckminster Fuller.* "Therefore it is important for our government to know if there are better ways of enclosing space in terms of material, time, and energy. If there are better ways society needs to know them." On the same page, he published an aerial photograph of Manhattan—with an enormous skybreak superimposed over midtown.

The picture could easily have been the cover illustration for a sci-fi novel.[5] In fact, it was produced for a 1959 exhibit at the Museum of Modern Art, where Fuller first advanced his proposal to build a skybreak a mile high and two miles in

---

4. A similar idea is now gaining popularity in Beijing, albeit as a matter of desperation. To shelter people from toxic air pollution, several companies have started selling inflatable "pollution domes." The largest of these transparent structures cover entire athletic fields and cost more than a million dollars.

5. Numerous science fiction novels have featured domed cities. As time has passed, and the genre has matured, doming has shifted from a utopian vision of an ideal future to a dystopian consequence of society gone amok.

diameter, enclosing some 250,000 people between 22nd and 64th Streets, from the Hudson to the East River. The vast scale was technically feasible because geodesic domes distribute load more efficiently as they get larger; they get stronger and proportionally lighter as their area increases. "In effect, the city would be one building," the MoMA architecture and design curator Arthur Drexler gamely explained.

Fuller was serious about the idea, and after it was politely passed over for New York's 1964 World's Fair, he advocated it whenever he had the chance. His fullest articulation came on September 26, 1965, when he wrote a three-page article for the *St. Louis Post Dispatch* titled "The Case for a Domed City."

The article argued that cities like New York are singularly inefficient in terms of energy consumption because skyscrapers have a large surface area that readily transfers heat. The warmth generated by radiators readily escapes in winter, as does the chill of air conditioning in summer. Fuller compared the spindly geometry of tall buildings to the fins on an air-cooled motorcycle engine. A dome is the opposite. "When we double the diameter of a dome, its surface area increases fourfold and its volume increases eightfold," wrote Fuller. "Therefore, each time we double the size of a dome, the amount of surface of the dome through which each molecule of interior atmospheric gas could dissipate its heat is halved; also, the number of molecules able to reach the surface in a given time is halved. . . . Due to the principle of energy conservation improvement with size, the larger the domed-over city the more stable its atmospheric conditions become, and at ever-decreasing cost per unit of volume."

Not that he expected to win mass support through geometry lessons. Comparing his dome to the skylighted arcades of Milan, his article described "the arcaded effect of a domed-over city in which windows may be open the year round, gardens in bloom"—a paradise with none of the inconvenience of dust, rain, or snow. Robotically actuated, the polarized glass panes would give complete control over the internal climate of the self-contained biosphere just by managing solar radiation and air currents. And if that wasn't enough, the dome would reduce "the radiation effects of neighboring regions' atomic explosions to below lethal or critical impairment magnitude."

It wasn't enough, at least not for blasé New Yorkers. The biggest skybreak Fuller ever built was erected in Canada, for Montreal's Expo 67, the World's Fair where he initially proposed to present his geoscope.[6] The internal climate of his 250-foot US Pavilion was controlled by 2,000 motorized acrylic panels. (The hexagonal windows were programmed to respond to the weather, providing shade or venting air.[7]) More than 5 million people visited. His dome was the Expo's signature attraction, but like most futuristic ideas at world's fairs, people perceived it as entertainment.[8]

Then one day in 1979, some city planners in Winooski, Vermont, reckoned that a dome was just what their town needed. Measuring 1.3 square miles, with a population of 7,500, Winooski wasn't exactly Manhattan—or even Montreal— but the planners were highly motivated: Winter temperatures routinely dropped below −20 degrees Fahrenheit in the economically depressed mill town, and energy prices were skyrocketing on account of the OPEC oil embargo. Initial estimates suggested that a dome would save residents as much

---

6. See Chapter 4.
7. This functionality was lost after the first day due to an electrical short.
8. Domes retain that image in the public mindset because they're most commonly seen in the context of entertainment, whether at Disney World's Epcot Center or the Eden Project's Biomes in Cornwall, England.

as 90 percent in heating alone. Winooski applied for $55,000 in research funding from the Department of Housing and Urban Development (HUD), and organized a symposium that Fuller enthusiastically attended. "In a time of growing population and dwindling resources, especially energy, it is incumbent upon technology to dedicate itself to provide mankind with the means of sheltering himself from the elements with the least amount of materials and resources," he declared.

Many locals were unconvinced. "What about nature?" someone asked a reporter from the *Christian Science Monitor*. "You can't interrupt nature like that. None of the birds would want to go south, and think of the pollution they would leave." When HUD rejected the funding request, the idea was quietly dropped.

The prospects for domed cities haven't really improved since Fuller's death. In 2009, the Discovery Channel's *Mega Engineering* series aired an episode titled "Saving Houston with a Dome." The show was purely speculative, with a level of hype befitting TV. ("Houston will set the standard for a new achievement in engineering, construction, and human ingenuity. As man seeks protection from climate change and faces an ever-changing world, cities could find new hope in a simple, strong, and soaring architectural triumph—a dome.") However, the engineers recruited by Discovery—including Fuller's former architectural partner Thomas T. K. Zung—took the challenge seriously. Considering the feasibility of construction (and durability during a hurricane), they concluded that a 21 million square foot dome most probably could be erected over downtown Houston using new materials such as ethylene tetrafluoroethylene (ETFE), and that careful regulation of solar radiation and convection currents probably would make Houston temperate.

"It may not be the dumbest idea ever, but it's close," retorted the *Houston Chronicle* when the episode aired. The Houston real estate blog *Swamplot* sarcastically asked for dibs on the thermostat. Instead of encouraging discussion or debate, the episode made most Houstonians defensive of their climate.

Engineers and visionaries like Fuller are prone to forgetting that cities are social constructs as much as they're constructed of steel and concrete. Cities have identities developed over decades or centuries. A total overhaul generally requires a natural disaster (like the 1906 earthquake in San Francisco) or an authoritarian mandate (like Georges-Eugène Haussmann's redesign of Paris under Emperor Napoleon III)—and neither San Francisco nor Paris was changed as radically as would be a city under a dome. So why not just start from scratch? Why not invent a new kind of city that has none of history's defects?

## III    Ecocities

IN ALMOST EVERY way, Abu Dhabi is the opposite of Winooski, Vermont. The capital of the United Arab Emirates (UAE)—source of 9 percent of the world oil reserves—Abu Dhabi is one of the wealthiest cities on the planet, and also one of the hottest. Summer temperatures can exceed 120 degrees Fahrenheit.

Cars and SUVs shuttle people everywhere, cosseting them from the outdoor heat. All buildings are air conditioned, chilling indoor temperatures to 60 degrees. The intense energy demand makes the UAE a net importer of natural gas, and gives Abu Dhabi the highest per capita carbon footprint globally. Even within this fantasyland of seven-star resorts and skyscrapers glimmering like newly minted money, the sultans and sheikhs realize that their extravagance isn't sustainable.

So back in 2007, Abu Dhabi committed $15 billion to build the world's first carbon-neutral city on 1,483 acres of empty desert approximately twenty miles from the capital. The city was given the name Masdar,[9] and the architect Norman Foster—Fuller's former associate—was hired to make it habitable to 40,000 people within a decade.

Foster proposed to set the whole city on a platform twenty feet above ground, with a fleet of driverless electric Personal Rapid Transit pods underneath. Swathed in solar panels, buildings would be heavily insulated against the heat, oriented to shade pedestrian walkways, and contoured to circulate air through the streets. Further cooling would be provided by a 146-foot-tall windcatcher in the city center.

The windcatcher is an ancient invention, found in the traditional architecture of Middle Eastern countries from Egypt to Iran. In one customary version, high-altitude winds are piped down to street level. In another, the phenomenon of warm air rising is exploited to draw heat skyward. With robotically actuated louvers, the Masdar windcatcher was designed to serve either function, depending on weather conditions, and also was assigned a third job: to display citywide power usage with an array of colored lights, broadcasting collective energy efficiency, maintaining public discipline.[10]

Though Foster's driverless transportation system was scrapped after the 2008 financial crisis, the wind tower has been erected, along with many houses. The combination of

---

9. *Masdar* means "source" in Arabic.

10. The architecture and placement of buildings are also based on historical precedents. Viewed in those terms, Masdar is less a source than a high-cost pastiche of traditional Middle Eastern communities overlaid with state-of-the-art solar power and many, many sensors.

shading and breeze keeps outdoor temperatures as much as forty degrees cooler than in Abu Dhabi. Still, the streets of Masdar are empty. The total population of the city is approximately 100, mostly students researching green energy at the Masdar Institute of Science and Technology. The remaining 39,900 residents are now expected by 2020, the latest estimate of when Masdar will be completed. But even if that many people can eventually be recruited, it will still be less metropolis than laboratory. (More than twenty Masdars would be needed just to house the population of Abu Dhabi City.)

And there's no reason to believe that the Masdar planners want anything other than an urban R&D lab in the Arabian Desert. "What we're learning at Masdar no one else knows yet," Sultan Ahmed Al Jaber, Masdar's managing director and CEO, boasted to *Time* magazine in 2011. "Masdar will be the global platform to test this technology."

The majority of so-called ecocities have just this ambition. In northern Portugal, for example, a company called Living PlanIT is planning a city to serve as a testbed for an "urban operating system" that will automatically optimize energy usage. Construed as a sort of company town housing the employees of Living PlanIT and its affiliates, PlanIT Valley will embed state-of-the-art green buildings with 100 million sensors. The sensors will be networked to provide real-time adjustments to the city infrastructure, controlling power and climate, and instantly dispatching workers in case of failure. Of course the sensors will also monitor residents' behavior.[11] The dream—or nightmare—of an urban operating system is that it will optimize people, much like the illuminated windcatcher in Masdar.

---

11. Living PlanIT is especially proud of a "Find My Child" app that promises to put the full power of ubiquitous surveillance at the disposal of parents concerned about losing a son or daughter at the mall.

However, the trouble with PlanIT Valley, much like Masdar, is that the most impactful innovations are tightly coupled, and therefore the least readily exportable. Parts of an urban operating system overlaid on an old city may make marginal improvements to legacy wiring and plumbing, but the game-changing potential lies in the disquieting omniscience of an electronic panopticon. Masdar is equally *sui generis*. What makes Masdar so remarkable is the overall shape of the city and how the topography optimizes wind patterns. In other words, if ecocities are to have a global impact and to accommodate the rapidly growing global urban population, they'll have to be mass-produced *in toto*, just like prefab houses.

That's the plan of Shimizu Corporation, one of Japan's largest construction companies. Since 2010, Shimizu has partnered with Nomura Securities to develop a modular system of marine cities called Green Floats.[12] Buoyant base modules would be manufactured on barges around the equator. Primarily comprised of lightweight magnesium captured from seawater, these honeycomb structures would be the foundations for circular floating islands, one kilometer in diameter, clustered in groups of three or more. Each artificial island would support a kilometer-tall tower, the upper section of which would house some 30,000 people together with business and recreational facilities: a "City in the Sky" where equatorial temperatures would be a mild 78 to 82 degrees Fahrenheit. Below this urban overhang would be industrial and farming facilities, with ranching at ground level and machinery to harvest energy from ocean currents

---

12. There is a long-standing fascination with floating cities in Japan—which occupied the collective imagination of the Metabolist movement for much of the 1960s—perhaps because the concept of offshore migration is a short leap for people accustomed to life on an island, and an alluring escape for those living in the congestion of Tokyo.

underneath. Shimizu engineers believe that such cities could be carbon negative: Total self-sufficiency, combined with the high efficiency of compact living in temperate urban towers, would make the Green Floats carbon neutral, and they could also carry technology to capture carbon from the atmosphere and sequester it in the surrounding sea.

None of this actually exists. Even the system to recover magnesium—which has a high natural concentration of 0.13 percent in seawater—has only been roughly approximated on paper. Nevertheless, Shimizu has already attracted a potential customer: The Republic of Kiribati.

Located in the Pacific Ocean near the equator, Kiribati is a collection of thirty-three islands with a total landmass of 313 square miles.[13] All but one are atolls, rings of coral reef with an average elevation of six feet above sea level. And the elevation is dropping as Arctic ice melts and global seas rise, leading the hundred thousand citizens to seek higher ground. One idea is mass migration to Fiji, but assimilation would effectively be the end of Kiribati. So the islands' president, Anote Tong, is in discussions with Shimizu. The company estimates that building the first floating nation would cost $500 billion—several thousand times Kiribati's gross domestic product—but that prices would rapidly drop if more Green Floats were built.

With Tuvalu and the Marshall Islands also in jeopardy—not to mention Florida—it could be a growing industry. "The idea behind the Green Float project was first as a solution to the problem of a rapidly growing human population," Shimizu general manager Masayuki Takeuchi told the *Telegraph* in September 2013. "But we quickly realized that it

---

13. Ocean is one resource that Kiribati has in abundance. Because the islands are spread out, the country controls a million square miles of the Pacific.

could save islands from rising sea levels." In fact, Green Floats are just one of Shimizu's construction schemes. The company has also released a conceptual blueprint for a "Mega-City Pyramid," a mile-high floating polyhedron spacious enough to host a population of one million.

## IV    Urban Tombs

NOT THAT A mile-high pyramidal city is an original idea. Buckminster Fuller first proposed one back in 1965, while his Manhattan Dome proposal was still in circulation. Like the Mega-City Pyramid, Fuller's Tetra City was designed for a million people, and, like Shimizu, he aimed to build the first of many in Tokyo Bay.[14] (His primary backer was Matsutaro Shoriki, a Tokyo media mogul whose end-of-life ambition was to house the world's population, starting with Japan.) "Three-quarters of our planet Earth is covered with water, most of which may float organic cities," Fuller wrote in *Critical Path*, where he pitched his idea in detail. "The tetrahedron has the most surface with the least volume of all polyhedra. As such, it provides the most possible 'outside' living. Its sloping external surface is adequate for all its occupants to enjoy their own private, outside, tiered-terracing, garden homes. These are most economically serviced from the common, omni-nearest-possible center of volume of all polyhedra."

In his 1970 book *The Pentagon of Power*, the architecture critic Lewis Mumford presented a less sanguine picture.

---

14. Admittedly, there are some differences. Shimizu's Mega City Pyramid is supposed to be a five-sided polygon, whereas Fuller's Tetra City was only going to have four sides. Also Tetra City was going to be powered by an on-board nuclear reactor.

Characterizing Tetra City as "a pyramid big enough to entomb the population of a whole town," Mumford's critique was more broadly a tirade against master planning in general—equally pertinent to cities in the sky and urban operating systems.[15] "There are many contemporary variants of such dehumanizing megastructures, apart from Buckminster Fuller's other project of a city under a geodesic dome: plans for underwater cities, underground cities, elevated linear cities, cities a mile high, all compete for attention as the City (read Anti-City) of the Future. Whatever their superficial difference, all these projects are essentially tombs: they reflect the same impulse to suppress human variety and autonomy, and to make every need and impulse conform to the system of collective control imposed by the autocratic designer."

Mumford wrote these words toward the end of an era of utopian architectural excess, as planned cities like Chandigarh and Brasília began to show their weaknesses. (Brasília's broad central avenues were monumentally empty of street life, concentrating poverty around the edges of town, where gang violence now rivals Rio de Janeiro.) And, if Brasília and Chandigarh weren't government capitals, it's questionable whether they'd even be inhabited. The smartest new "smart cities," like Songdo in South Korea, are as hard-pressed to attract residents as Masdar. Built from the ground up at a cost of $35 billion, Songdo has ubiquitous videoconferencing and pneumatic garbage disposal, but city planners can't fill even 20 percent of the commercial office space.

Jonathan Thorpe, one of Songdo's developers, told the BBC that "it's the occupants who make a city" in a 2013 interview, an obvious point that suggests why urban planning

---

15. More than anywhere else, Mumford's book should be reprinted in China, where more than one hundred "model cities" are planned.

is anything but obvious. Anticipating how hundreds of thousands of people will interact in a future urban environment is nearly as chancy as predicting how future climate conditions will respond to geoengineering. Since future human behavior cannot be adequately predicted, a planned city must either break those who live in it or be broken by them. Neither option is appealing. If only for that reason, predesigned cities are unlikely ever to be more than living labs or rescue rafts for climate refugees.

Real cities *are* a human invention, but they're invented and reinvented by everyone who lives in them. They're products of the human variety lauded by Mumford, the collective wisdom he appreciated in the contour of medieval streets that broke cold winds, or the orientation of donkey paths that optimized local transportation.[16] Yet Mumford was wrong to group Fuller's Dome over Manhattan with Anti-Cities of the Future, to equate it with Tetra. Like Fuller himself, Mumford was blinded by the glimmering geodesic structure.

## V    Metroengineering

IN THE WINTER of 2011, engineers began drilling boreholes into ice sheets atop the Tuul River in Ulan Bator. The city suffers notoriously frigid winters, during which temperatures can drop to −40 degrees Fahrenheit. But ice is an insulator, so the solid surface of the Tuul keeps the water below warm enough to remain liquid. The holes allowed engineers

---

16. The former Fuller enthusiast Stewart Brand has provocatively taken this notion to an even greater extreme in a 2010 essay for *Prospect* magazine titled "How Slums Can Save the Planet." Taking a close look at shantytowns from India to Brazil, he writes that "the magic of squatter cities is that they are improved steadily and gradually by their residents. To a planner's eye, these cities look chaotic. I trained as a biologist and to my eye, they look organic."

to flush water to the surface, where it froze and thickened the river's ice cap. By repeatedly pumping up water and letting it freeze, the engineers increased the thickness of the cap to as much as twenty feet.

Working on behalf of the Mongolian government, the engineers were artificially replicating a process observed in Siberia, where spring water seeps through cracks in surface ice to create a layered ice sheet known as a naled. Some Siberian naleds are so thick that they never melt. The Mongolian engineers wanted to make one hefty enough to last through the summer months, when temperatures can reach as high as 100 degrees, and have been rising each year at a rate of three times the global average. They were building an air conditioning unit for the city, a mass of ice that would cool the breeze.[17]

The experiment worked, and the engineers believe that artificial naleds could serve as cold sinks in many other cities with continental climates, from China to Finland, where winters are long and annual temperature variation is extreme. It's a low-profile urban retrofit with a high impact. In summer months, naleds can moderate the local climate—much as Buckminster Fuller sought to do by putting cities under skybreaks.

The notion of doming cities was never really about domes in their own right. Although Fuller was infatuated with geodesics—and collected royalties every time a dome was built—his primary motivation was to enclose the most space with the least material, or, more broadly, to control the most space with the least infrastructure. He articulated

---

17. As in many cities, summer warmth is exacerbated by a phenomenon known as the urban heat island effect, where the energy used to run air conditioning pushes temperatures even higher.

it best in a widely quoted 1967 newspaper interview about his Montreal dome: "The pavilion can be regarded as a prototype environmental valve,[18] enclosing sufficient space for whole future communities to live in a benign physical microcosm though still situated and visually related to a hitherto climactically hostile environment."[19] For Fuller, a shelter was nothing more or less than a microclimate. Architecture was just thermodynamics.

Skybreak domes and naleds are only two of many technologies for valving, controlling how weather flows through a city day by day and from season to season. Taichung Gateway Park in Taiwan, currently in development, will provide a range of microclimates artificially optimized for different activities, including sports and relaxation. While some of the technologies have a long history—such as fountains that chill the surrounding air with their mist—others are still experimental. For instance, the tropical climate will be moderated with dehumidifiers, dropping the perceived temperature by an estimated six or seven degrees.

Other technologies have already been installed in Athens, a city where power consumption typically doubles in summertime due to air conditioning. When Flisvos Park was renovated in 2010, University of Athens researchers replaced the dark asphalt with paving stones pigmented to reflect over 70 percent of infrared sunlight. That simple intervention cooled the park by approximately three degrees in the hottest months. The same research group has since combined reflective paving with geothermal heat exchangers, which pump

18. For Fuller the former seaman, the meaning of *valve* was very broad. For instance, in a 1973 lecture to students at Harper College in Illinois, he characterized skiing as "angular valving of gravity."

19. Of course the ultimate microcosm is a spacecraft, which helps to explain what Fuller was thinking when he observed that "the answer to the housing problem lies on the way to the moon" in a 1966 interview with *The Washington Post*.

air through underground pipes to moderate temperature. (Because earth is a good insulator, subterranean temperatures remain nearly constant throughout the year. Winter air pumped underground is warmed, and summer air is cooled.) In summer months, this combination of techniques keeps Flisvos Park seven degrees cooler than before.

And technologies are getting more sophisticated. One of the most promising is thermochromic tile. Designed to change color with temperature, thermochromic paving gets lighter in warmer weather and darker in cooler, alternating between reflecting and absorbing heat from the sun.

Because every city has a unique geography and history, each will require a unique combination of strategies to attain the "Garden of Eden interior" that Fuller once promised, but that his all-purpose skybreaks were too simplistic to provide. In effect, each city will need to be climatically tuned like an engine or musical instrument. As with geoengineering, the process will not be entirely predictable, but the limited scope will make mistakes reversible and improvements incremental.

Metroengineering has the potential to make almost every city temperate without burdening the global climate. Making more cities more temperate will make them more attractive to more people, eventually sequestering most of the world population in carbon-neutral cities. And as the global climate stabilizes, metroengineering will become easier, making local climates ever more temperate. Eventually, most cities should be clement enough for the people within to spend most of their lives outdoors. The function of walls and roofs will become increasingly psychological rather than physiological: an architecture of social structures, as mutable as notions of privacy and propriety, within an intangible environmental envelope.

Buckminster Fuller should have foreseen it. After all, his technological worldview was formulated during World War I, when he observed technology moving "from the track to the trackless, from the wire to the wireless," as he phrased it in *Education Automation*. This is the process he called *ephemeralization*, and he regarded the progression from mortar and bricks to geodesic domes to be one of his great contributions. Evolution from the dome to the domeless is the next logical step. With their metroengineered microclimates, cities can reinvent shelter by reducing or eliminating the need for it.

# 6

# PEACE
## The World Game

## I   Gaming Vietnam

IN THE SPRING of 1964, as fighting escalated in Vietnam, several dozen Americans gathered to play a game. They were some of the most powerful men in Washington: the director of Central Intelligence, the Army Chief of Staff, the National Security Advisor, and the head of the Strategic Air Command. Senior officials from the State Department and the Navy were also on hand.

Players were divided into two teams, red and blue, representing the Cold War superpowers. The teams operated out of separate rooms in the Pentagon, role-playing confrontation in Southeast Asia as simulated in a neutral command center. Receiving each team's orders, the commend center's experts modeled the interplay of blue and red moves, and issued mock intelligence reports in response. Reports reflected the evolving conflict, but the intelligence was intentionally distorted to replicate the fog of war. After days of playing out different scenarios, the war gamers reached the conclusion that civilians in the United States and the rest of the world would vocally protest an American bombing offensive.

The need to anticipate the dynamics of conflict increased as the U.S. Congress passed the Gulf of Tonkin Resolution in August, effectively declaring war on North Vietnam. So another war game was played. This time the teams included more high-ranking officials, including the Deputy Secretary of Defense and Assistant Secretary of State. Defense Secretary Robert McNamara was an active observer.[1]

The objective was to play out the situation in Southeast Asia six months in the future, with the premise that North Vietnamese troops had destabilized the South, Chinese advisors were working on North Vietnam's behalf, and American soldiers were starting to perish. After ruling out an American nuclear attack, the teams role-played their way to quagmire, in which the North Vietnamese countered every US move in spite of lives lost and ruined infrastructure. The games forecast political crisis in the United States, with no plausible path to American military victory. For the second time in a year, war games proved prescient, and also futile, as the government insisted on letting tragedy play out for real.

Buckminster Fuller foresaw the consequences of American intervention in Vietnam without the help of a military simulation. As America went to war, he warned the United States Information Agency (USIA) that worldwide regard for the nation would soon be "at its lowest ebb in many decades, if not in the total two centuries of the USA's existence." This was real cause for concern, since the Cold War was being waged on the basis of public image

---

1. The list of participants in the Sigma I and II war games is a veritable who's who of the Vietnam era, including McGeorge Bundy, William Bundy, Cyrus Vance, John McCone, Earl Wheeler, and Curtis Lemay. In *Wargames*, military historian Martin van Creveld aptly observes that "except perhaps for a few medieval tournaments, probably in the whole of history no higher-ranking group of men had ever played a wargame of any kind."

as much as physical power, and the USIA was responsible for American propaganda. However, Fuller had a solution, and he believed it could be implemented by as early as 1967, in time for the Montreal World's Fair. His idea was simple: Instead of playing secret war games deep inside the Pentagon, the United States should host a world peace game out in the open.[2]

The concept was an elaboration on his proposal to build a geoscope inside the US Pavilion. An animated Dymaxion world map would show all the resources on the planet, as well as all human and natural activity, from troop deployment to ocean currents.[3] On this map, the world's leaders and citizens of all nations would be invited to publicly wage peace. "The objective of the game would be to explore for ways to make it possible for anybody and everybody in the human family to enjoy the total earth without any human interfering with any other human and without any human gaining advantage at the expense of another," he wrote in *How It Came About (World Game)*. "To win the World Game everybody must be made physically successful. Everybody must win."

The rejection of Fuller's plan by the US government only further convinced him of its urgency for the whole planet, impelling him to spend the rest of his life pitching computerized world games to audiences ranging from the Senate to the Kremlin, and experimenting with

---

2. Though the specifics of the Sigma games were secret, the American public was aware that war games were being played by the government. Most people had learned about these politico-military games in 1963, when a brief vignette showing "mock war in the lower level of the Pentagon" was included in Milton Caniff's syndicated comic strip, *Steve Canyon*. Caniff was a favorite of the military, and was frequently used by the Pentagon to leak information.

3. The Expo 67 geoscope is more fully described in Chapter 5. Fuller proposed to build the geoscope inside a geodesic dome as a globe that would unfold.

"long-hand" versions in university classrooms. He insisted that world games were a remedy for war because they were the antithesis of war games, and an antidote to "zero-sum" game theory. "Game theory, as outlined by the late Princeton Professor, John Von Neuman [*sic*], is employed by all the powerful nations today in their computerized reconnoitering in scientific anticipation of hypothetical world wars III, IV, and V," Fuller told the Senate Subcommittee on Intergovernmental Relations in 1969. "[T]he theory of John von Neuman's war gaming, which holds that ultimately one side or the other must die, either by war or starvation, is invalid."

The Pentagon-funded RAND Corporation, where the majority of Cold War game theory and war-gaming were developed, returned the volley, fully concurring that Fuller's world-gaming was the opposite of their methodology. One 1972 RAND review called Fuller's writings and Senate testimony "a potpourri of pitchmanship for an ill-conceived computer-based game" that would "retard real progress in the field".

Yet for all the good reasons Fuller and RAND had to be wary of each other, their differences were never as sum-zero as they professed, and in the years since the Cold War, the relationship between games of war and peace has only grown more nuanced. There is now better reason than ever to trust Fuller's instinct that games can help "make the world work"—to use one of his favorite phrases—and greater cause than ever to realize his vision for a world game. However, success will require all of the wisdom that can be drawn from war games and the commercial gaming industry spawned by Pentagon technology. It will also take something that the 1964 war games so obviously lacked: the willpower to act on what gaming can teach.

## II    Chessmen and Nuclear Warheads

WAR GAMES ARE as ancient as gaming, and as primordial as war. Some of the most archaic games from China and Greece, such as *weiqi* and *petteia*, modeled the tactical movement of soldiers. And chess, the ultimate game of strategy, is a direct forerunner to the Pentagon's Cold War simulations.

In its ancient Indian form, chess was called *chaturgana*. The game was played with markers signifying infantry, chariots, horses, and elephants, all overseen by pieces representing a vizier and monarch. Winning required the destruction of the opposing army or the capture of the king, much the same as in real battle at the time. While the game became less martial in outward appearance as it spread to Persia, China, and Europe, military men seem not to have been distracted by queens and bishops. The game provided mental training for commanders ranging from William the Conqueror to Tamerlane.

However, traditional chess, even when played with chariots and elephants, had obvious differences from battle. The opposing armies of chessmen were completely identical and the terrain was perfectly uniform, making the conflict artificially symmetrical. Moreover, both sides had total knowledge of the entire battlefield, including all enemy positions. Orders were implausibly orderly, carried out instantaneously as each player politely took his turn. And there were no external factors akin to disease or storms. Chess was a closed system. Chaos and chance were eliminated.

This level of abstraction had obvious advantages. The purity of chess allowed players to focus on the grand challenge of anticipating an opponent's behavior while upsetting the opponent's expectations. But since strategic choices were never so stark in war, the most a commander could expect from chess was sharpened intellect, and there was always the threat that a young warrior would misunderstand what was being simulated and expect troops to obey as placidly as chess pieces.

Beginning in the seventeenth century, European military strategists considered ways in which to make chess conform more closely to real fighting so that chess could provide more well-rounded training. At first it was just a matter of enlarging the battlefield and making armies more varied, with markers representing cavalry, artillery, and infantry. By the eighteenth century, the squares of the gameboard came to represent different kinds of terrain, either by varying their color or by transferring the grid onto a regional map. Rules were written to vary the speed at which troops advanced based on whether they were on horse or foot, and whether they were crossing meadows or scaling mountains. Players were also responsible for rudimentary logistics, ensuring there were supply lines to keep soldiers fed.

But that was just the beginning. The full transformation from chess to *kriegsspiel* occurred in the nineteenth century, when a Prussian lieutenant named Georg von Reisswitz layered in aspects of a sandbox game invented by his father. The elder Reisswitz's game was played with ranks of toy soldiers engaged in mock combat, where the outcomes of ambushes and battles were decided by dice. (The results of each dice throw were tallied according to real battlefield statistics specifying the range of casualties to be expected in any given scenario.) The young lieutenant replaced his father's sandbox battlefield with a flat topographic map, across which markers representing companies and units could be advanced at the rate permitted by the terrain. As in real warfare, neither side had total knowledge of the conflict. Each played on a separate board, with an umpire making his way back and forth. Rules derived from battlefield experience determined how much the umpire allowed each side to see of the opposition. Those rules also guided the dice-thrown results of combat.

The verisimilitude of *kriegsspiel* impressed some of Prussia's highest-ranking officers, including the chief of staff, Helmuth von Moltke, who made the game central to officer training by periodically bringing the War College out to the Prussian border in order to game hypothetical enemy invasions. The game would be played on a map corresponding to the surrounding landscape. Precise data for each maneuver would be collected by marching the local garrison through the formations on the gameboard. On this basis, Moltke not only provided training but also supplied tactical plans for the garrison in case of actual invasion.

Yet as the realism of *kriegsspiel* increased, the rules governing it—and the effort of playing it—threatened to overwhelm war-gaming. Partly this was a practical issue: The more time required to set up and play out a scenario, the smaller the number of scenarios that could be explored. But there was also the deeper risk that greater verisimilitude would paradoxically make gameplay less relevant. It was the opposite of the issue with chess, where the lessons learned were universal yet abstract. In *kriegsspiel*, the lessons were often so concrete as to be *sui generis*. And even if the perfect occasion arose for applying a war-gamed tactic, the complexity of *kriegsspiel* made it difficult to determine whether the results were biased by how the rules interacted.

In 1876, one of Moltke's officers, Colonel Julius von Verdy du Vernois, proposed an alternative: Replace the rules with the judgment of experienced umpires. *Free war games*, as they were known, could be played in two adjoining rooms with nothing more than a pair of topographical maps and two sets of markers. The umpire passed back and forth between teams, collecting orders and providing intelligence. Instead of using charts, players used their instinct to estimate how fast troops could advance, and the outcomes of battles were decided—without dice or casualty tables—at the umpire's own discretion. This arrangement made the games fast, like actual warfare, and the umpire knew the reason for his decisions, which meant he could help players to understand the outcome at any level of abstraction: The game was a prelude to discussion. Though Reisswitz-style games continued to be played, Verdy's influence was profound. His free *kriegsspiel* established a continuum from rigidity to openness, just as Reisswitz's rigid *kriegsspiel* established a continuum from abstraction to realism.

Games could be configured at any point along these two axes, optimized according to what the commander wished to achieve. And as war-gaming developed, expectations increased. Games could be used for training officers, building camaraderie, identifying leaders, understanding enemies, anticipating conflicts, inventing tactics, testing strategies, predicting outcomes. In the United States, where *kriegsspiel* was imported in 1887, one of the first questions was logistical. The Naval War College gamed different scenarios to determine whether fuel supplies for battleships should be shifted from coal to oil.

In Europe, *kriegsspiel* was widely used to develop strategies for ground war. Given Prussian tradition—and German delusions of grandeur—Germany was especially active, developing whole file cabinets of battle plans. One of the most promising played out the invasion of Holland and Belgium in order to quash the French army before the British could assist. The game determined that Germany would triumph against France as long as ammunition could be rapidly replenished. For this purpose, Germany built the world's first motorized supply battalions, deployed in 1914. And the plan might have worked brilliantly, if the only players had been the German and French armies. But the German *kriegsspiel* failed to factor in the pride of Belgian civilians, who proved ready and able saboteurs—even of their own railroads—upsetting German momentum. Even more catastrophic, the game left out diplomacy, which, by way of alliances, brought the United States into the war—and not on the side of the Reich.

The defeat of Germany in World War I suggested the need for another dimension in war games: a sociopolitical axis. Depending on the circumstances, war games needed to model the non-military implications of military actions, and to do so from the local to the global scale. Only when all three axes were properly accounted for could a game function meaningfully. And the appropriate level of abstraction, openness, and inclusiveness were different for every situation and every purpose.

All the major militaries gamed at multiple levels in the interwar period, with varied results. Germany successfully used war games to invent the blitzkrieg, Japan gamed the maneuvers their navy would later use to occupy Pacific island outposts, and the United States gamed the amphibious tactics that distinguished the Marine Corps. But games delving into politics were more treacherous because more variables were less accountable. Free games played by Germany in the early 1930s—in which participants included diplomats, industrialists, and journalists—failed even to protect the Weimar Republic from internal collapse. In Japan, the Total War Research Institute held political-military games in 1941 that simulated the political interests and military power of countries including the Soviet Union, Great Britain, and the United States. The games correctly predicted a Japanese defeat of England in the Far East, incorrectly anticipated a German victory over the Soviet Union, and utterly discounted the resolve of the United States.

Arguably the United States used war games most effectively in World War II because the US military was most attentive to their limitations. A postwar assessment by Admiral Chester Nimitz provides some insight into the American approach: "The war with Japan had been [enacted] in the game room here by so many people in so many different ways that nothing that happened during the war was a surprise—absolutely nothing except the Kamikaze." In other words, the United States wasn't presuming to predict the future—to simulate geopolitics fraught with unknown unknowns—but rather was creating a vast database of short-term hypotheticals, an industrial-strength version of what Helmuth von Moltke once had attempted in Prussia. American gaming explored the problem space of war in the 1940s, and the games produced heuristics. The only limitation was the American military imagination, which was simply too American to conceive of Japanese suicide missions.

This exploratory approach was carried forward into the Cold War, reinforced by the circumstances of nuclear armament. The fundamental problem faced by both the US and Soviet militaries in the 1950s and 1960s was aptly summed up by the RAND physicist Herman Kahn. When his expertise was questioned by military officials, he'd retort, "How many thermonuclear wars have you fought recently?"[4]

The nuclear era was entirely unprecedented, and one wrong decision could cause the end of civilization. There was

---

4. Kahn was one of the chief inspirations for Dr. Strangelove. (John von Neumann was another.)

thus an urgent need to explore absolutely every eventuality, while acknowledging that many eventualities couldn't possibly be foreseen. The Pentagon gamely simulated Josef Stalin's sudden death and a Soviet first strike on Inauguration Day. The purpose of this free gaming was generally heuristic: Since a good model would need to account for everything in the world—given that nuclear war was inherently global—good models were all but unbuildable. Instead the Pentagon opted for many inadequate simulations and gave low credence to any of them. In the words of one Navy analyst, gaming was a "training device for aiding intuitional development." RAND referred to it as "anticipatory experience."

Yet inevitably US government and military leaders wanted to master the Cold War. They sought victory over Communism. Advances in game theory and computing stoked that ambition.

Around 1954, RAND analysts began to consider how von Neumann and Morgenstern's *Theory of Games and Economic Behavior* could be applied to warfare. They started by mathematically modeling campaigns from World War II, working out how opposing armies should have acted. And if fighting tactics from the past could be optimized, then why not future planning for nuclear engagement? In 1960, Harvard economist Thomas Schelling explored the possibility in a book called *The Strategy of Conflict*. His book took up von Neumann and Morgenstern's non-zero-sum games, showing that in an age of mutually assured destruction, the United States and the Soviet Union could both win, with no risk of loss, if only they exercised mutual restraint.[5] This was an

---

5. Which isn't to say that Schelling was a peacenik idealist. For instance, he argued that the appearance of recklessness could be advantageous. He compared it to teenagers playing chicken.

excellent solution, except there was no obvious way to apply it: neither a framework for trust nor the political will to see the adversary benefit. The level of abstraction at which game theory was viable made the most compelling conclusions practically irrelevant. In that sense, it was like chess.[6]

At about the same time that Schelling published his book, the US military acquired a computer devoted to war-gaming. Installed at the Naval War College at a cost of $10 million, the Naval Electronic War Simulator had no game theory in it. Rather the machine was a sort of electromechanical umpire, managing data and calculating dice throws for role-playing games. Later versions had a similar function, though one side or both might be played by the computer itself, allowing the gaming process to be greatly accelerated. Countless games could be played, countless options considered, countless outcomes recorded. If game theory was the *non plus ultra* of chesslike abstraction, these computerized simulations were the ultimate extreme of Georg von Reisswitz's *kriegsspiel*: resolutely concrete and hopelessly vulnerable to programming biases.

For strategic purposes, game theory was too vague and computer simulations were too specific. The most versatile and insightful technique remained the oldest still in use: the nineteenth-century free war games of Julius von Verdy du Vernois.[7]

If only they could provide more than heuristics. (Legitimate skepticism about their predictive value may partly explain why gaming had so little sway over US policy in Vietnam.)

---

6. Given the inherent abstraction, game theory was increasingly marginalized in practical military planning even as it became popular shorthand (and a favorite Fuller synonym) for military intelligence.

7. In twentieth-century military jargon, free games were referred to by the formidable acronym BOGSAT. It stood for *Bunch of Guys Sitting Around a Table*.

An early intimation of what free war games could become was suggested by Attorney General Robert Kennedy in 1963. After playing a politico-military game organized by Schelling, Kennedy inquired about gaming a resolution to racial inequality in the South: an alternative to political debate in which all interests could role-play their way to civil rights. The idea was abandoned following President Kennedy's assassination, but a permutation arose in 1970, when MIT political scientist Lincoln Bloomfield traveled to Moscow. As a guest of the Soviet government, Bloomfield orchestrated a simulation where Soviet, American, and Israeli officials unofficially war-gamed a hypothetical Middle East conflict akin to the Six-Days War.[8] Bloomfield intentionally scrambled their positions. The pro-Arab Soviets played Israel, and the anti-Soviet Israelis and Americans played the Soviet Union. In these topsy-turvy circumstances, the Soviet "Israelis" surprised everyone by developing a policy of moderation.

So what if all nations were involved, and simulated all the issues dividing them? That's what Buckminster Fuller really sought when he proposed his world game at Expo 67. With everyone playing together, they wouldn't have to predict the future. They could create it by consensus.

## III   Everybody Must Win

LIKE AMERICAN WAR games, Buckminster Fuller's world game originated in the Navy. "Navy is world," he often asserted. "Army is local." What he meant was that the world's oceans

---

8. Bloomfield was a pioneer of Cold War–era war-gaming, frequently consulting with the RAND Corporation and the US government in the late 1950s. At around the same time, he started to develop what he called "peace games," foreshadowing Fuller's world game by half a decade.

are all interconnected—really the same body of water—and therefore any viable naval strategy must be global. Moreover, the fundamental strategic problems are logistical. "Who's going to control the line of supply?" he asked rhetorically in *Everything I Know.* "That's who's going to control the world."

Fuller's understanding of naval supply lines, learned during his officer training at Annapolis, was coupled with his admiration for Henry Ford, whose success he attributed to total mastery of materials and manufacturing. To keep his assembly lines running smoothly, Ford needed to know the global availability of raw materials from iron to limestone and how quickly they could be transported by ship or rail. "His complete inventory was in motion," Fuller explained. "He developed a world game strategy very much the same way the Chief of Naval Operations [knows] where all our ships are." Of course Ford's world game, much like the Navy's logistical war-gaming, was predicated on competition. It was a means of attaining dominance. What Fuller started thinking about was logistical coordination for the benefit of all: If everyone shared lines of supply equitably, as overseen by the total coordination of world-gamed design science, the battle for control would be neutralized. Political and economic warfare would become irrelevant.

Precisely when Fuller began thinking in these terms is debatable. Beginning in the 1960s, he claimed to have been world-gaming since 1927, the year of his mythical lakeside epiphany. Without question, the housing he began developing in the late 1920s had some nautical qualities—in terms of mobile self-sufficiency—and one of the selling points was that they could be built by assembly line. There was also a strong emphasis on technological efficiency and a latent concern for materials, from the exotic alloys that would replace heavy brick to the waste packaging toilet that would recycle excrement as fuel. Perhaps there was even the suggestion of collective problem-solving, or at least a self-organizing principle at work: With the portable Dymaxion house, people could spontaneously distribute themselves on Earth where the resources they needed were readily found.[9]

So by the late 1920s, Fuller was at least sensitive to the issues that would motivate his world game. But it was only after he was hired by the Phelps Dodge Corporation in 1936 that he began to seriously consider where materials were naturally deposited on the planet and where they were needed. Specifically he thought about copper, since copper mining was Phelps Dodge's main business. He analyzed the amount of copper in the ground, the rate at which it was mined, and the average time span of use before it was scrapped. On that basis, he was able to make forecasts for the company, predicting when there would be a shortage or surplus. And since copper was used so widely by so many industries, copper circulation predicted demand for all elements. Fuller's research was thus the raw material for applying his understanding of Navy logistics to human needs in general.

He began to chart that explicitly in 1940 while working as a technical consultant on the tenth anniversary issue of *Fortune*. The issue was dedicated to showing that the decade-long Great Depression was coming to an end, and his task was to establish that the United States was poised to lead the world in industrialization.[10] He did so by comparing resources and production in the United States to the rest of the world, showing for instance that "each man in the United States" had an 87 percent share of the global iron

---

9. For details on the Dymaxion house, see Chapter 2.
10. Conceived by Henry Luce in 1929, *Fortune* was launched just three months after the stock market crashed, and endured the Great Depression by championing capitalism to the few people wealthy enough to afford its dollar-an-issue cover price.

ore, a 95 percent share of petroleum, and a 97 percent share of motor vehicles. He also charted "progress" from 1850 to 1940, showing the annual per capita growth in the number of radios, telephones, and airplane seats—all on the rise—and the escalating efficiency of alloys and engines. "By industrialization we built a new civilization," proclaimed the unsigned text accompanying Fuller's charts. "And during the last fifteen or twenty years, by further industrialization, we have created the possibility of an entirely new era for mankind."

Clearly the article was polemical, combining nationalistic competitiveness with a paternalistic call to "help raise the standard of living of the rest of the world." How much of this reflected Fuller's thinking in 1940 may never be known, though Fuller's voice permeates the most utopian passages. ("[Industrialization] has created a new kind of life, augmented and hitherto unimagined.") What was most important to Fuller in the long run was the relationship between materials and technology: the idea that technological advances effectively increased the amount of available materials by decreasing the quantities needed to build a bridge or circumnavigate the world. He'd always believed it. His *Fortune* research gave him the numbers to tout it as scientific fact.

And then there was the archive in its own right, reams of data that *Fortune* gave Fuller when the magazine moved offices in 1945. The statistics became the foundation of his World Resources Inventory. With that personal database, he began the private game of matching up planetary supplies and demands. Given the political and economic constraints of his era, his game was pitched to the future. (A chart he drew in 1952 plotted exponential technological acceleration since the year 1900, predicting a world fully provided for by the turn of the millennium.) In Fuller's future, politics would be technologically obsolete, and resources could be managed with total technocratic efficiency as dictated by the design science of world-gaming. The only trouble was that any world in which the world game could realistically be implemented was a world in which world-gaming would be superfluous.[11]

Fuller's 1964 proposal to the United States Information Agency was his most inspired attempt to overcome that impasse. By directly involving the people who could enact the results of gameplay, he cast the world game as a political system, a completely democratic alternative to voting in which people collectively played out potential solutions to shared problems. Granted, he never articulated it in those terms. He was too deeply invested in anti-political rhetoric. ("War is the ultimate tool of politics," he wrote with characteristic zeal in his 1967 manifesto, *Utopia or Oblivion*.) Nor was there any chance of implementation by a governmental organization chartered to promote the national interest. His world game depended on "desovereignization," a point he illustrated with a vivid military metaphor. "We have today, in fact, 150 supreme admirals and only one ship—Spaceship Earth," he wrote in *Critical Path*. "We have the 150 admirals in their 150 staterooms each trying to run their respective stateroom as if it were a separate ship." Those supreme admirals embodied geopolitics for Fuller, and his world game was indeed an alternative to their warring—or might have been if only he had a global platform.

The platform he got was more parochial. At the New York Studio School, there were no world leaders or computers. Instead, over a six-week period in the summer of 1969, Fuller assembled twenty-six college students from sixteen

---

11. Fuller was also always faced with the problem of explaining why, if progress toward utopia was inevitable—as predicted by his charts—any effort to get there was necessary.

disciplines—including anthropology, biology, and physics—
to game the greatest problems facing the planet.

He started by lecturing about his ideas for two weeks.
Then he had the students work with his ever-growing World
Resources Inventory to survey where resources were located,
where they were desired, and what trends could be expected
to affect supply and demand. Guided by Fuller's principles, the students calculated the "bare maximum" of human
requirements—such as the amount of protein and electrical
energy needed for someone to live comfortably—and displayed these needs by population density on a sixty-foot-
long Dymaxion map. Their next task was to optimize the
planet.

On one level, it was the freest of free games, effectively
free of gaming. On another level, it was the most rigid game
ever, since the student output was precisely the input that
Fuller gave them in his preliminary indoctrination. They
uncritically accepted his technocratic premise, and embraced
his long-standing opinion that the highest planetary priority
was a world energy grid, reiterating his data and recapitulating his reasoning: Electricity was the common requirement
of all modern technologies, from transportation to farming,
and populations stabilized when electrical power was available because human labor was no longer needed. High-
voltage lines carrying solar power around the world could
freely supply sufficient energy to everybody at all times. (It's
always sunny somewhere on the planet.) With a power grid
following the continental layout of Fuller's Dymaxion map,
life everywhere would be improved and all bare maxima
would be met.

Peerlessly rational, it was typical world-game reckoning,
and superficially it looked like a marvelous achievement.
Reporting on the proceedings for the radical *Los Angeles*

*Free Press*, Gene Youngblood declared that "a concrete scientific alternative to politics now exists." Yet the Studio School yielded no new insights (such as how to physically build the hypothetical grid, or how the US and USSR could be convinced to share power). Even Fuller grew wary of the seminar format. In a 1971 report titled *World Game Series: Document One*, he reframed the 1969 games as "simulated explorations" intended to make participants "realize individually by personal experience that they, too, were suddenly realistically envisioning that all of humanity could become not only physically and economically successful, but that this could be accomplished within decades." In other words, the world game seminar was recast as pedagogy.[12]

Fuller fully exploited the pedagogical value. He trademarked WORLD GAME, restricting it to seminars that he supervised. The seminars served to indoctrinate new disciples, who were told that only he understood the underlying design science.

At the same time, Fuller lobbied for funding to build the computer he believed real world-gaming required. In 1969 he told the Senate that the mainframe would cost $16 million (a staggering $6 million more than the Naval Electronic War Simulator). Like the Navy's machine, its main function would be to manage data and to umpire gaming scenarios. Sometimes he also endowed it with the ability to collect information: a sort of disembodied worldwide panopticon. He justified the high cost by describing the difficulty of gaming the whole world. "The processes consist of mathematical

---

12. Fuller's biographer Hugh Kenner more snidely described these seminars as tending "to turn into encounter groups." They may even have been detrimental, convincing large numbers of student activists to share his false and unsubstantiated beliefs. For instance, increasing the efficiency of farming could as easily lead to a population increase. (Recent research shows that the only reliable way to make people have fewer children is to raise the standards of education.)

procedures not only as incisive and complex as those involved in celestial navigation, or astro-ballistics, or the space program, but even more so," he wrote in his introductory memorandum to the *World Game Series: Document One*. Given the size of the world population, "the World Game is seven times more complex than China's quarter century industrialization and thirty-five times more complex than was Russia's industrialization problem."

But complexity was only the half of it. The other half was credibility. His prodigiously expensive computer could set the world's 150 supreme admirals on the same course because they'd trust it. They'd trust it even if they couldn't trust one another. Computers were "opinion-proof," he claimed. They had none of the flaws of human judgment. For instance, computers controlled airplane flight. Everyone who'd ever flown had outsourced their survival to electronics, and tacitly accepted that computers were more reliable decision-makers than human pilots. If they had entrusted their lives to a computer, then why not the fate of the planet? As he argued in *How It Came About (World Game),* "No human beings can persuade other people to behave in various unfamiliar, untried ways . . . but any one of us can yield becomingly to the computer."[13]

And his computer would be "photogenic." With data visualization capabilities drawn from his geoscope, it would be perfect for prime time television. (He even claimed that this would help to pay for it, estimating that the world media rights would be worth $2 million.) Watched by all, the celebrity computer would persuade the billions of its electronic

---

13. *How It Came About (World Game)* was formally submitted to the *Congressional Record* as part of Fuller's Senate testimony. Though the hearing was not about Fuller's world game computer, his testimony was really a thinly veiled appeal for money.

wisdom, imposing popular pressure on politicians. The admirals would have to accept their new leader. He dubbed the world game a "world brain."

The years passed, and the computer remained unbuilt. Without a machine to constrain him, Fuller grew increasingly vague about the world game. By the time he published *Critical Path* in 1981, *world game* had effectively become an alias under which he passed off whatever he believed, rendering his ideas indisputably opinion-proof. He became the world brain, using *world game* more capriciously than the royal *we*: "World Game finds that the computers fed with all the relevant energy-efficiency facts will be able to demonstrate which uses will produce the greatest long-term benefit for all humanity," he wrote. In other words, the computer that did not yet exist was preemptively validating itself.

The truth is that Fuller's digital panacea would never have worked, since, as all war gamers know, all war games involve compromises. The universality of abstraction comes at the expense of realism. Models that are more reliable are less comprehensive. Games of greater complexity are less intelligible. The rules that make games more objective are themselves subjective. The problem is compounded by the complexity of a computer program, where biases may be too deeply embedded to be detected by anyone. For war game designers, there's at least the compulsion to avoid personal prejudices, since one of the core values of gaming is to understand the opposition. Fuller's objective, blatantly obvious from his behavior in seminars, was to validate his own assumptions. A computer could be programmed to do that, and bright flickering lights could make it telegenic, but it wouldn't have revealed anything more profound than what Fuller had already written.

At best, it would have optimized the solutions he'd already given. The bare maxima of life, as defined by his criteria, could be calculated to a few extra decimal places. The cables of his global power grid could be configured to several percent greater efficiency. But certainly nothing original—like the idea of a bare maximum or globalized power supply—would have been generated by the machine or humans interacting with it. His computer would have been a more precise and compliant version of his seminar students.

In his Senate testimony, Fuller distinguished the world game from war games by comparing world-gaming to mountain climbing. "[T]he object would be to find all the moves by which the whole field of climbers would win as each helped the other so that everybody successfully reached the mountaintop," he said. "This is a mathematically permitted alternative of game playing but it has never been played in any of the war games of the great nations of the earth."

Fuller's climbing metaphor is revealing because it shows his confusion about gameplay: All games are challenging, but not all challenges are games. Whereas the challenge of scaling a mountain requires that each participant reinforce the decisions made by fellow climbers, the decisions made in a game are independent and deliberately subverted by fellow players.[14] The ordered volatility of a game, the regulated collision of conflicting intentions, brings participants to what Lincoln Bloomfield called "unforeseen choice-points" in which each choice is a discovery.

---

14. The underlying weakness of Fuller's approach is well known to computer scientists by another clambering metaphor: *hill climbing*. The pursuit of a local optimum excludes global exploration. (There's *still* an organization, the Global Energy Network Institute, trying to implement Fuller's half-century-old idea.)

As Bloomfield showed in Moscow, choice-points can serve peace as well as conquest. The underlying reason that war-gaming entails competition is not because competition is bellicose but because it's creative.[15] Fuller's world game could be won, and it still can, but only if it's made as creatively playable as *chaturgana* and *kriegsspiel*.

## IV  Everybody Must Game

IN 1953, A former Army infantryman named Charles Roberts designed a simple war game for civilians. *Tactics* was played on the map of a fictitious landscape. Akin to Reisswitz's *kriegsspiel*, there were tables to calculate casualties and counters to represent battalions. The self-published game sold well enough for Roberts to found a company, Avalon Hill, which launched the recreational war-gaming industry.[16]

Will Wright started playing Avalon Hill war games as a teenager in the early 1970s. A decade later, as personal computers became commonplace, he decided to program a game of his own. *Raid on Bungling Bay* didn't appear as cerebral as the Avalon board games he'd played. On the surface, it was a first-person shooter embedded in a flight simulator. But Wright had incorporated a sort of military-industrial realism, in which the targets chosen by a player impacted enemy capabilities. The way to win was not to develop better reflexes, but to intuit the dynamics of weapons manufacturing and supply chains.

---

15. Beginning in the 1950s, war games became popular strategic and training tools for businesses. By the early 1960s, many major corporations—including Chrysler, General Electric, Bell, and Boeing—were regularly using war-gaming to improve their competitiveness. The popularity of business war games has since only increased.

16. There were predecessors, most notably *Little Wars*, published by H. G. Wells in 1913. As a committed pacifist—and an accomplished satirist—Wells proposed that opposing generals play his game instead of warring, leaving everyone else to live in peace.

Wright's next game dispensed with reflexes entirely. In *SimCity*, the player was mayor of a make-believe municipality, responsible for managing the urban dynamics of sustenance and growth. Crucially, there was no preordained goal. The player set personal standards of what the city should become and strove to make the sim conform to that vision. As in any real city, it wasn't easy. (Attract companies by lowering taxes and the decline in social services may raise crime rates, driving away business.) The deep causal loops that made *kriegsspiel* so compelling were brought into the civilian realm, introduced to a single-player context where the conflict was internal. *SimCity*'s urban scaffolding could support endless variations: Like *kriegsspiel*, it was not a specific game but the logical framework for gaming. Wright has described it as a "possibility space" in which the player becomes the game's designer, and the design of a game is a design for society. *SimCity* and Wright's later creations—so-called *god games* including *SimEarth* and *Spore*—provide a link between the tensions of war games and the intentions of Fuller's world game.[17]

Another link was emerging around the same time that Wright was transitioning from Avalon Hill to Bungling Bay. At the University of Essex in 1978, two students, Roy Trubshaw and Richard Bartle, programmed a multiplayer adventure game for the campus computer network. The text-based role-playing game was the first of its kind, a sort of dungeons-and-dragons quest open to anybody who logged on to the mainframe. Trubshaw and Bartle called their creation *Multi-User Dungeon*, or *MUD*, a name that became the moniker for a whole genre of network-based

---

17. Other god games of the period, such as Sid Meier's *Civilization*, are also pertinent, though most are more structured than *SimCity*.

adventure games, especially once the Internet networked everyone.

As advances in computing passed from the military to the commercial sector, the MUDs that followed *Multi-User Dungeon* evolved from text-based interaction to graphic exploration. These online environments invited discovery and conquest. Players could collaborate or compete. They could build together or kill each other. Eventually these modes of online engagement drifted apart. The collaborative impulse led to virtual worlds, including *Second Life,* populated by player-controlled avatars that keep house, socialize, and dabble in virtual sex. The competitive drive resulted in massively multiplayer online games (MMOs) such as *EverQuest* and *World of Warcraft*, in which avatars go to battle and collect loot.

The number of people who participate in virtual worlds and MMOs is staggering. At its peak, *Second Life* hosted 800,000 inhabitants—nearly the number of people living in San Francisco—and *World of Warcraft* reached a peak population of 12 million. Beyond the sheer numbers is a remarkable level of commitment. *Second Life* contains well over 100 million user-created objects—from houses to garments—and more than \$3 billion worth of in-game currency has changed hands since the virtual world launched in 2003. (Spent on virtual objects and real estate, the money retains real-world value, tradable for dollars through a company-managed financial exchange.) In *World of Warcraft*, launched in 2004, players have created more than 500 million characters, nearly twice the population of the United States. They have also documented every facet of gameplay, producing the second largest wiki after Wikipedia.

While luring hordes of strangers to interact online has proven relatively easy, getting them to do so sustainably has been more challenging. The problem was evident as early as 1986, when LucasFilm invited 500 people to try out a virtual world called *Habitat*. Players rapidly tired of organized activities such as chess tournaments, so the game designers gave them swords to play with. Mass bloodshed ensued, as players ruthlessly murdered one another for fun. *Habitat* was swiftly shut down.

The anarchic violence was even more extreme a decade later with the launch of *Ultima Online*. The MMO immediately attracted 50,000 players, who promptly went on a rampage, killing off all flora and fauna before turning on each other. Those who survived became thugs, killing off newcomers. The only way game designers could control the carnage was to set up a separate server for newbies in which homicide was disabled. Ever since, computer code has become the standard defense against player abuse, far easier to impose than community standards.

Nevertheless, the sheer number of participants in virtual worlds and MMOs has inspired some commentators to look at *World of Warcraft* adventurers and *Second Life* denizens—as well as an additional 500 million active gamers worldwide—as an ideal labor pool to save the world. As Institute for the Future researcher Jane McGonigal argued in her 2011 book, *Reality Is Broken*, gamers are "our most readily engagable citizens." McGonigal sees gaming as a platform for world-changing, proposing to "use everything we know about game design to fix what's wrong with reality." At least in spirit, the 'serious games' that she and her colleagues advocate are both a reflection and extension of Fuller's vision.

Yet few "serious" games have engaged gamers in substantial numbers for significant time spans. With names like *World Without Oil*, serious games tend to be prescriptively frontloaded—much like Fuller's world game—well-intentioned positive reinforcement for true believers.[18]

One exception is *America's Army*, a military training MMO built on a commercial game engine licensed by the Pentagon.[19] Released to the public as an Army recruiting tool, the fast-paced first-person-shooter has attracted more than 10 million players. It's a classic example of "militainment," allegedly instilling military values such as honor, but really just providing the perennial thrill of fighting.

Another exception to foreboding seriousness—an example more pertinent to promoting peace—is the god game genre. God games are massively popular. (Will Wright's titles alone have sold nearly 200 million copies.) But they have never really fit the massive multiplayer format, since the premise of a god game is omnipotence, which logically cannot be shared. Electronic Arts, the publisher of *SimCity*, tried to split the difference with an online multiplayer re-release in 2013. (Cities remained autonomous, but could trade and collaborate on "great works.") The awkward combination of antithetical genres quite naturally provoked a backlash. *SimCity* cannot become what it was never meant to be. What's needed instead are games designed from the start to allow a massive multiplicity of players to interact in open-ended possibility spaces.

Crucially, these virtual worlds would not be neutral backdrops in the vein of *Second Life*. Like *SimCity* and war games, they'd be logically rigorous and internally consistent. There

---

18. That hasn't stopped McGonigal, who created *World Without Oil*, from anticipating big results. Discussing *World Without Oil* in *Reality Is Broken*, McGonigal writes, "It was a proof-of-concept game that convinced me we really can save the real world with the right kind of game. It's the project that inspired me to define my biggest hope for the future: that a game developer would soon be worthy of a Nobel Prize." Certainly a worthy goal.

19. The Pentagon now licenses most game technology from industry. For instance, *Second Life* is the platform for many virtual training exercises.

would be causality and consequences, and there would be tension, drawn out by constraints such as limited resources and time pressure. Also like *SimCity* and war games, these virtual worlds would be simplified, model worlds with deliberate and explicit compromises tailored to the issues being gamed. There could be many permutations, and should be, so that none inadvertently becomes authoritative. The only real guideline for setting variables would be to adjust them to breed what Wright has described as "life at the edge of chaos."[20]

Within these worlds, scenarios could be played out by the massive multiplicity of globally networked gamers. Players wouldn't need to be designated *red* or *blue*, but could simply be themselves, self-organizing into larger factions, as happens in many MMOs. Scenarios could be crises and opportunities. For instance, imagine a global financial meltdown that destroys the value of all government-issued currencies, provoking the United Nations to issue a "globo" as an emergency unit of exchange. Would the globo be adopted, or would private currencies quash it? And what would be the consequences as the economy was rebuilt? A single universal currency might be a stabilizing force, binding the economic interests of people and nations, or it could be destabilizing on account of its scale and complexity. It could promote peace or provoke war. Games allowing players to collaborate and compete their way out of crisis would serve as crowdsourced simulations, each different, none decisive, all informative.

Informative to whom? To the gamers, first and foremost. And as the number of players increased through the evolution of world-gaming, the outcomes of these games would inform an increasingly large proportion of the planet. At a

---

20. Good game design happens to correspond to the state of the world.

certain stage, if the numbers became great enough, game-play would verge on reality—and even merge into reality—because players would collectively accumulate sufficient anticipatory experience to be able to play their part in the real world more wisely. Whole aspects of game-generated infrastructure—such as in-game companies and NGOs—could be readily exported since the essential relationships would have already been built. Games would also serve as richly informative polls, revealing public opinion to politicians with unprecedented nuance.

Or they could play a more direct role in governance. The unstated idea nascent in Fuller's Expo 67 proposal—that gaming could serve as an alternative to voting—could potentially be realized were a plurality of people gaming national and global eventualities. For any given issue, different proposals could be gamed in parallel. As some games collapsed, gamers would be able to join more viable games until eventually the most gamable proposal was played through by all. That game would be a surrogate ballot, the majority position within the game serving as a legislatively or diplomatically binding decision. Provided that citizens consented from the start, it would be fully compatible with democratic principles—and could break the gridlock undermining modern democracies.

When Buckminster Fuller presented the world game as a method of brokering global concord, he wasn't ambitious enough. The act of gaming must itself make peace.

# THE RANDOM ELEMENT

*The Buckminster Fuller Legacy*

# I   The Acolyte

IN THE SUMMER of 1972, *Life* magazine sent a photojournalist across the United States to document the newest housing boom. From New York to California, John Dominis photographed geodesic domes, showing the creative ways people adapted to "living in the round." The photographs were featured in an eight-page spread, accompanied by an article noting that "domes and domelike structures of all shapes, sizes and materials are popping up on the landscape like mushrooms after a rain."

Of all the many examples, the one most prominently featured belonged to a California builder named Lloyd Kahn, who'd made it by hand in the hippie town of Bolinas. "In an ordinary square house, vitality just sits down and dies in the corners," he told *Life*. His dome was edgeless—a single large room built of recycled wood with an expanse of Plexiglas looking out on forest—enlightened living through architecture. So that everyone could live as he did, he'd authored two books, bestselling guides that translated Buckminster Fuller's industrial engineering into do-it-yourself shelter for the people.

Kahn was one of Fuller's most ardent followers. Trained in old-fashioned big-timber building, he'd been converted to geodesics in 1967, when he heard Fuller lecture at the Eslan Institute in Big Sur. He was persuaded by the ecological advantages of lightweight construction, enthralled by Fuller's idea that waste could be eliminated by design. As he later wrote to Fuller, he began making dome homes with "the Design Science Revolution foremost in mind." He published his *Domebooks* in part to increase the number of hands-on revolutionaries, but also (as he noted in *Domebook 1*), to inspire a broad range of "prototypes for future industrial production of low-cost housing."

Toward that end, Kahn frequently experimented with materials. Constructing the buildings for an alternative Northern California boarding school, he made panels of sheet metal, fiberglass, ferrocement, vinyl, and polyurethane foam. The domes were built with students, on a budget of just $1,200 apiece, and erected in just a few months to beat the winter rains. Even more than Kahn's Bolinas retreat, they embodied the potential of geodesic domes as accessible and affordable shelter. Within a couple of years, they also embodied the problems.

The structures expanded and contracted as temperatures changed. Given the complex geodesic geometry, and the need to cover each facet with a separate panel, the buildings started leaking all over the place. Exacerbating the problem, the most appealingly lightweight materials—such as fiberglass and vinyl—deteriorated in sunlight.

Observing the damage, Kahn began to reconsider the merits of geodesic shelter. By late 1972, he had stopped printing *Domebook 2*, and had written a rambling renunciation. "Metaphorically, our work on domes now appears to us to have been smart: mathematics, computers, new materials, plastics," he wrote in *Smart But Not Wise*. "Yet reevaluation of our actual building experiments, publications, and feedback from others leads us to emphasize that there continue to be many unsolved problems with dome homes. . . . We now realize that there will be no wondrous new solution to housing, that our work, though perhaps smart, was by no means wise." Kahn clearly felt betrayed, and he responded by vigorously challenging "the assumption, encouraged for a time in my mind by Bucky Fuller, that we will have to depend upon new technologies, new materials, new designs to solve the housing crisis on an overpopulated earth." He proclaimed that plastics were poisonous, that producing them was environmentally reckless, and that the industry that made them belonged to Richard Nixon. Just months after *Life* presented him as the man bringing domes to the masses, Kahn recast himself as an advocate of all that Fuller rejected. "In the past year, we have discovered that there is far more to learn from wisdom of the past: from structures shaped by imagination, not mathematics, and built of materials appearing naturally on the earth, than from any further extension of whiteman technoplastic prowess."

Even after Fuller's death, Kahn continued to denounce his former hero. "Mamas, don't let your mathematicians grow up to be builders," he warned in a 1989 manifesto titled *Refried Domes*, and in a 2012 *BoingBoing* interview he groused about "problems with Buckminster Fuller's ideas," asserting that "they weren't really the kind of ideas that I was in favor of." Over that span of thirty years, he'd become one of the foremost advocates of indigenous architecture, documenting the construction of yurts and mud houses, log cabins and thatched cottages, all of which utilized local materials to meet the needs of life in their environs. He claimed that these vernacular designs were more practical and ecologically sound than plastic-paneled domes, a point that would be hard to dispute were one to compare the thatched cottages in an Irish village to a geodesic boarding school in the Santa Cruz mountains.

Kahn was right to question Fuller's hype. Geodesic domes are not universally appropriate. (In most cases they're about as suitable for housing as a log cabin on the Mongolian steppe.)[1] However, the geodesic dome was just one end product of

---

1. That said, yurts and mud huts are hardly appropriate in a city. While Kahn should be commended for leveraging past wisdom, past wisdom is all but useless for compact urban living.

Fuller's design science revolution. Geodesic construction was an example of design science, not its underlying principle. What mattered was the effort to design holistically for the greater good of Spaceship Earth. Ultimately the geodesic dome was as dispensable as the Dymaxion car or the Wichita House.

Lloyd Kahn's polemics miss this essential point. Building geodesic structures didn't make Kahn a comprehensive anticipatory design scientist, and identifying the problems with domes didn't threaten design science as a whole, nor did it imply that all good ideas come from the pre-industrial past. Kahn's connection to Fuller, both positive and negative, was totally superficial.

In that respect, Kahn is typical of Fuller's followers, which says something about them and still more about Fuller himself. For all his talk of guinea-pig openness, he didn't really tolerate dissent. Though he frequently contradicted himself or changed course, at any given moment he was so totally convinced of his worldview—from first principles to minor details—that alternatives were meaningless. From Black Mountain workshops to World Game seminars, Fuller always lectured and never argued, leaving little space in his life for anyone but unquestioning acolytes. These intellectual shadow puppets came and went, contributing nothing to his design science revolution other than the appearance of a movement.

And then he was dead. That made him easier to venerate or vilify or forget. His personal legacy has proved perfectly adequate for his cult of personality, and his artifacts have become retro-futurist baubles for a new generation of designers to ogle. At their best, his inventions provide points of origin for contemporary innovation, as they have done in the preceding six chapters. But what about the legacy that matters most? What about the legacy of comprehensive anticipatory design science?

## II   The Independent

NOT ALL OF Buckminster Fuller's admirers were acolytes. Some, such as Frank Lloyd Wright and Arthur C. Clarke, simply appreciated the radical thinking of a kindred spirit. Far rarer were the independently articulating friends who shared Fuller's commitment to comprehensively solving the world's great problems, but without following his methods or condoning his solutions.

"Independently articulating" was Fuller's description of his friendship with Victor Papanek, as he characterized it in his introduction to Papanek's seminal *Design for the Real World*. "There are wonderful friendships which endure both despite and because of the fact that the individuals differ greatly in their experiential viewpoints while each admires the integrity which motivates the other," Fuller wrote. "Such friendships often are built on mutual reaction to the same social inequalities and inefficiencies. However, having widely differing backgrounds, they often differ in their spontaneously conceived problem-solution strategies. Victor Papanek and I are two such independently articulating friends who are non-competitive and vigorously cooperative."[2]

Papanek's background had more in common with Lloyd Kahn's than with Buckminster Fuller's, at least in terms of his interest in other cultures. Papanek and Kahn were both

2. Papanek returned the complement in his book, expressing his admiration for "men like Buckminster Fuller who spend 100 percent of their time designing for the needs of man." He also kept a Dymaxion world map in his office.

explorers, traveling the world to observe the lives of people living independently of "whiteman technoplastic prowess."[3] However, unlike Kahn, Papanek had the formal training of a designer, and the conviction that—as he wrote in *Design for the Real World*—"design must become an innovative, highly creative, cross-disciplinary tool responsive to the true needs of men."[4] Repudiating Fulleresque techno-utopianism, Papanek was deeply disturbed by the environmental damage wrought by designers in the twentieth century. (He believed that "industrial design has put murder on a mass-production basis.") But he claimed that was because designers had failed to develop their world-changing capacity; they didn't use their power responsibly. The design profession was focused too much on designing alluring products and not enough on "the social and political environment in which design takes place."

Papanek's travels took him everywhere from Alaska to Indonesia, and each cultural encounter expanded his conception of design. He wasn't especially concerned with documenting artifacts or craftsmanship, and he certainly had no intention of cataloguing pre-industrial material culture for wholesale imitation by post-industrial back-to-the-landers. What he picked up was more fundamental. Living in an Eskimo village, for instance, he learned an alternative way of perceiving space—aural rather than visual—which helped locals to navigate flat Alaskan tundra. "Nonlinear, aural space perception imposes fewer vertical and horizontal limitations on the Eskimos' world-view," he observed in *Design for the Real World*. His Eskimo acquaintances seemed to be

---

3. Fuller traveled many more miles than both of them put together, but it was never in the spirit of discovery, always to proselytize.

4. As a young refugee from prewar Vienna, Papanek apprenticed with Frank Lloyd Wright and studied at Cooper Union and MIT.

completely indifferent to visual orientation. Their homes were often decorated with magazine pictures hung sideways. They could read upside-down. For Papanek, the insight was not that magazine design should be more eclectic—as a literalist like Kahn might conclude—but rather that designers should rigorously assess the cultural blocks limiting their perception of problems and solutions.[5] (One example reminiscent of Fuller's Dymaxion bathroom: Overcoming the Western fecal taboo, Papanek proposed to decrease pollution and energy consumption by converting human excrement to fuel.)

To fix the world's ills, Papanek did all he could to make design thinking global. Yet he was equally emphatic that thoughtful design was specific to a place and people. There was no cosmic Dymaxion widget that would make mankind a universal success. Global design thinking had to be grounded in local conditions.

That was another motivation for Papanek's travels. In 1960s Indonesia, for instance, he found villages so isolated that people had no access to outside information. Since the people were illiterate, he realized that any communication would have to be verbal, and the only practical way to communicate verbally would be by radio. For radio, there had to be electricity. That wouldn't have phased Buckminster Fuller, who'd most likely have presented the Indonesian government with his master plan for a world energy grid.[6] Papanek had a rather different reaction. For millennia, people in Southeast Asia had burned dried dung for heat. The warmth, he determined, was sufficient to produce minimal

---

5. Papanek looked at world cultures much as Fuller viewed the cosmos. His anthropology was as unreliable but as personally enriching as Fuller's cosmology.

6. And the grid would be sufficient to power his two-way TV, conveniently sheltered from the monsoons by placing Indonesia under a geodesic dome.

voltage across a thermocouple, a simple device made by connecting two wires of different metals. If the radio was reduced to a coil, an earplug, and a few other basic components, the thermocouple would provide sufficient power to pick up any signal in the region. The radio would have none of the refinements an American consumer might expect. There wouldn't even be a tuner. But with only one signal likely to reach Indonesian villages at any given time, tuning wouldn't matter. What was important for Papanek was that the radio could be made by local untrained labor at a cost of nine cents per unit and—housed in a used tin can—could be locally maintained for decades.

Papanek was castigated by colleagues for designing something so ugly; his prototype used an upside-down juice can bristling with bare wires. Ugliness was a professional taboo. Couldn't he at least apply a coat of paint? Papanek countered that the purpose of his invention was to let villagers affordably access information. Those were the pertinent design criteria—reflecting the social and political environment— and in any case he had no right "to make aesthetic or 'good taste' decisions that will affect millions of people in Indonesia." The plainness invited them to make the radios their own, which they did by embellishing the cans with bits of glass and shell. "This is a new way of making design both more participatory and more responsive," he proclaimed in *Design for the Real World*.

That was an overstatement—both grandiose and patronizing—but at least it was a beginning. Over the following decades, Papanek increasingly backed away from the role of designing artifacts for others, preferring to play the part of mediator. Sharing his training and experience, he could bring the benefits of global design thinking to any group anywhere in the world. He could support their process of defining and addressing local problems as only they could do for themselves, and after he left, their designs could continue evolving independently of him.

On the surface, Papanek's mediation was the opposite of Dymaxion universalism. Yet Fuller himself recognized that he and Papanek shared a core belief that aligned their efforts to improve the human condition. "Victor Papanek speaks about everything as design," he approvingly wrote in his introduction to *Design for the Real World*. In his final chapter, Papanek elaborated on this theme, using language that deliberately echoed Fuller's terminology. "Design [is] the primary, underlying matrix of life," he wrote. "Integrated design is comprehensive: it attempts to take into consideration all the factors and modulations necessary to a decision-making process. Integrated, comprehensive design is anticipatory. It attempts to see trends-as-a-whole and continuously to extrapolate from established data and interpolate from the scenarios of the future which it constructs."

In other words, Papanek practiced comprehensive anticipatory design science. He was as legitimately a comprehensive anticipatory design scientist as Buckminster Fuller. The design science revolution could—and did—have more than one protagonist. There has been—and remains—more than one mode of implementation.[7] And this is more than just a historical detail. Arguing that every designer should become a polyglot, Papanek asserted that "the structure of languages gives us ways of dealing with and experiencing realities, each discreetly different in each language." The same can be said for the distinct design languages of Fuller and Papanek.

---

7. Yet another approach can be found in the contemporaneous architecture of Paolo Soleri, whose densely layered city plans were based on the "logistical perfection" of living organisms. Fuller deemed Soleri "one of the greatest of the dreaming strategists."

Knowing more than one expression of design science fosters independent articulation.


## III   Corporate Interests

IN JANUARY 2014, Google acquired Nest Labs for $3.2 billion. The four-year-old company manufactured just two products, updated versions of humdrum home appliances: the smoke detector and the thermostat. The Nest devices were undeniably stylish. The thermostat was awarded a gold medal by the Industrial Designers Society of America, and was added to the permanent collection of the Cooper-Hewitt National Design Museum. But these were not the principal reasons for Google's multibillion dollar purchase. The Nest gadgets abetted Google's effort to make every house a smart home—a seamless physical extension of the Internet.

A Nest thermostat learns inhabitants' preferences and habits by analyzing behavioral patterns, automatically controlling heat and air conditioning for an optimal climate. For example, the heater might power down during work hours, turning on as people head home. A smartphone app provides remote control in case of an unexpected visit. And the thermostat interfaces with the Nest smoke detector, disconnecting heating appliances if there's carbon monoxide in the air.

The interaction between devices, and interactivity with inhabitants, are the bases for Google's excitement. Nest is a model for enriching all home appliances with machine learning, networking them, and connecting them to the cloud, where Google can provide an online platform for total home optimization.

Google is also working to optimize transportation. Alluring for their hands-off convenience, driverless cars may eventually be coordinated as efficiently as web traffic. A computerized car can learn passengers' habits and preferences—not unlike Nest's thermostat—and can interface with other vehicles for a smoother commute. Sharing the same platform as smart homes will improve the performance of both, and both can be further enhanced with wearable computing: The smart home and driverless car belong to the same seamlessly augmented reality as Google Glass.

Is Google the future of comprehensive anticipatory design science? Without question, the company has anticipated a future more comprehensively designed than Buckminster Fuller ever imagined, and is scientifically developing every component to be globally implemented.

The environmental benefits could be dramatic. Nest claims to lower heating and cooling bills by 20 percent since appliances run only when required, and energy companies offer rebates because the thermostat makes power consumption more consistent. A Google platform for the entire home in every home on the planet would vastly increase efficiency, and total integration with a smart grid would stabilize energy demands, facilitating conversion to renewables such as solar and wind. The advantages of eliminating traffic are even more obvious: Lower energy usage and less pollution—especially if the cars run on hydrogen—not to mention the public health benefits of diminished stress and fewer collisions.

The technocratic Buckminster Fuller would surely have approved. He was eager to cede control of world affairs to computers, the ultimate goal of his world game. Nor did privacy issues concern him, as he made clear when he lobbied for an omniscient geoscope. Fuller's comprehensivism called for big solutions to big problems. His proposed dome over Manhattan had all the daring and whimsy of a Google moonshot. He was as comfortable with military funding and as manic for patents as any venture capitalist. He placed great faith in corporations, venerating Henry Ford and collaborating with Kaiser Aluminum.

And if Google somehow didn't appeal to him, the twenty-first century offers many more options for a corporate design science revolution. "In this connected age, no company can stay bound to 'I'm just going to make this one piece of the puzzle,'" Nest CEO Tony Fadell told *Fast Company* shortly after selling out to Google. He mentioned Samsung, Apple, Amazon, and Microsoft as competitors to control our technological future. Any of them could engineer an ultra-efficient infrastructure. But is this the version of comprehensive anticipatory design science we should buy?

As Victor Papanek showed, there's more than one way of conceiving a design science revolution. The version that connected him to Fuller certainly wasn't the vision driving Google and Samsung. To begin with, Papanek was adamantly opposed to patents. More deeply, the simplistic equation of anticipatory comprehensivism with technological efficiency ignores the social and political environment in which design takes place. Corporations are not environmental stewards or humanitarian organizations. They may underwrite environmental or humanitarian initiatives for marketing purposes, top managers may be genuinely philanthropic, and profitable business practices may bring benefits to the public, as Google has done with web search. However, the purpose of a corporation is to compound shareholder investment. That is what every company is designed to do. Corporate comprehensivism is inherently monopolistic. Any anticipatory activity is inherently predatory. Corporations are not inherently good or evil; they're inherently corporate. The comprehensiveness of their vision is limited by the framework of capitalist competition.

What makes Fuller so endlessly compelling is his Dymaxion inconsistency. He was both corporate and anti-establishment, and more concerned with making the world work than with resolving his internal contradictions. The future of design science depends on Fulleresque pragmatism. It will require corporate innovations, given the ubiquity of corporations, yet corporate ubiquity must simultaneously be resisted in order to maintain the integrity of design science in its own right. Design science revolutionaries must critically consider all paths to world-around comprehensiveness, lest we reduce *doing more with less* to back-to-the-land fantasy or bottom-line efficiency.

## IV    The Practice

SO HOW DO you foment a revolution? How do you make the world work for 100 percent of humanity, in the shortest possible time, through spontaneous cooperation, without ecological offense or disadvantage to anyone? How do you become a comprehensive anticipatory design scientist? Reconsider what Buckminster Fuller sought, with an independence befitting Victor Papanek.

### Biomimesis

With more than 3.5 billion years of evolution, nature is the world's most experienced problem-solver. It's also the most comprehensive, since all life shares the same biochemistry, every species interacts with all others through natural selection, and all of life collectively comprises a single biosphere. Yet every organism is independent, each species autonomous. There are myriad adaptations to innumerable niches on a planet that is anything but homogenous. Life is striking for both its variety and its cohesiveness. Together, these qualities have made life versatile enough to flourish in deserts and tropics and deep-sea vents, and have rendered life resilient enough to survive massive asteroid strikes.

The attentive designer draws on both of life's strengths—variety and cohesiveness—when confronting a problem. The comprehensive anticipatory design scientist integrates them with such deftness that the solution seems practically to be alive in its own right.

Variety is the easier of these traits to take up, which is why it's more typically enlisted. Life can be viewed as a vast catalogue of solutions to problems posed by the world we live in. Mobility is an example, and fish and birds have both evolved ingenious modes of transit. These are appropriated in traditional biomimesis. The result is a Bionic or Dymaxion car—or George Cayley's nineteenth-century airships.

Cohesiveness is approached by observing living interactions. Life can be seen in terms of networks such as food webs, or can be viewed even more abstractly in terms of nitrogen, methane, and carbon cycles. Cohesive design begins by considering how species relate to each other, and then applies these relationships in human society. To an extent, this is the approach Buckminster Fuller took up when he envisioned zoomobiles providing humans the freedom of wild ducks. Ostensibly learning from waterfowl, he was proposing seasonal human nesting as an alternative to fixed urban planning, regional identities, and national animosities.

To combine cohesiveness with variety requires that the design scientist consider network and nodes simultaneously, the interrelationships and individual adaptations of all species within a niche. Or at the very least, it requires the design of a system in which cohesiveness and variety can coevolve, where there are enough rules for the former and there is enough flexibility for the latter. The World Wide Web is the closest that humanity has come to this ideal—and it's no coincidence that the Web seems more alive than any other human invention. The challenge for future comprehensive anticipatory design scientists will be to reach beyond the Web, an accidental breakthrough that, for all its comprehensiveness, certainly was not anticipated to become what it is today.[8]

The cohesiveness and variety of nature can prepare ambitious comprehensive anticipatory design scientists to reinvent deeply troubled human ecosystems such as banking and international relations. The designer should seek to redefine individual roles by drawing inspiration from the variety of life, and seek to redefine relationships by drawing inspiration from living systems.[9] Our knowledge of biology is extensive and is growing exponentially. What we need is comprehensive anticipatory biomimesis.

## Adaptability

The first machine for living was the cell membrane. In order for life to evolve, oceans of self-replicating nucleic acid needed to be portioned into living units isolated by containers of lipid. These packages of RNA could compete, and the most successful could replicate. Natural selection could get started.

Over time, the membranes became complex, efficiently absorbing nutrients and excreting waste. In some cases (such

---

8. In the beginning, the web linked elite scientific institutions, using protocols initially developed for military communication.
9. Consider the potential of resource cycling, discussed at the end of Chapter 1.

as amoebae), cytoskeletons provided mobility. In others (such as nematodes and chimpanzees), the membrane mediated intercellular communication and collaboration, the basis for multicellular organisms. Some of those organisms (such as the donkey) powered the first human machines. Those human machines (such as the plow) powered civilization, facilitating organization into towns and cities. Is it any wonder that a machine-driven society should be intent on reconceiving the home as a machine for living?

Buckminster Fuller's forays into housing were cellular in many respects. His Dymaxion houses were complex membranes to contain the American nuclear family. Modular units, frequently mobile, they were selectively permeable protective coverings that could be replicated in quantity. There's no good reason to believe that they were deliberately biomimetic. Their relationship to comprehensive anticipatory design science, rather, is that, like cells, they were adapted to living. They were not designed to show off wealth or to appear homey. An essential starting point for comprehensive anticipatory design science is to clearly identify the problem and to develop a solution that addresses that problem as appropriately as possible. Natural selection imposes that pressure on life. Fuller attempted to impose it on himself.

Yet, for all their comprehensiveness, Fuller's homes were not sufficiently anticipatory. Such is also the case with an amoeba, which is exquisitely evolved for the present, not for the future. In his homes, Fuller sought amoeba-like perfection, and his Wichita House came close to achieving it before changing housing conditions rendered his invention obsolete. His particular amoeba could not survive. However, amoebae in general—and life in general—*are* anticipatory, because adaptations are transitory. Their ability to evolve is the anticipatory aspect of their design.[10] The comprehensive anticipatory design scientist must be attentive to changing conditions: Change is certain to happen. Equally certain, the specific changes are unpredictable. The designer must therefore also be a metadesigner, designing for adaptability, even at the expense of flawlessness.

## Convergence

Education is specialization. Such has always been the case, and often with reason. Apprenticeship prepares the blacksmith to practice his perilous craft. Through military training, cadets become infantrymen, interchangeable in death. A PhD in particle physics or neuroscience requires at least a decade of focused study, culminating in further specialization after the doctorate is awarded. Even the apparent exceptions to specialized education don't look so exceptional on re-examination. The arts drill students in theory, and the humanities specialize students in the liberal arts canon.

Undoubtedly our knowledge of the world has increased with specialization, as has our ability to alter our surroundings. Any solar physicist knows more about the sun than Galileo did, and any hydrologist can move water more effectively than Archimedes could. Specialization has facilitated this knowledge gain since the specialist is specially positioned to leverage past research. But more knowledge mandates more specialization. It's a positive feedback loop that Buckminster Fuller recognized could have a negative impact on society because people would be conditioned by their

---

10. Consider the idea of self-generating houses, proposed in the final section of Chapter 2.

specialty. Our scientifically informed technological world is spectacularly complex. Specialists cannot comprehensively study the world's problems, and cannot anticipate the impact of their solutions outside their own specialty. In that respect, specialized training is anathema to comprehensive anticipatory design science. The comprehensive anticipatory design scientist specializes in convergences.

Fuller was an autodidact whose self-education was guided by his naive curiosity. The initial impetus for his two-way TV was to provide an open resource for unstructured autodidactic study. It was both a brainteaser and a mental prosthesis: a brainteaser because new ideas might emerge from the chance meeting of disparate information in a curious mind, and a mental prosthesis because it could deliver specialized knowledge on demand.

Resources far more vast than Fuller ever imagined are now available to anyone with an Internet connection. The English-language Wikipedia alone includes nearly five million articles, enough to sustain a quarter century of nonstop reading—which would be pointless since Wikipedia is always changing. Information is increasingly pervasive and increasingly unstable.

Any dedicated comprehensive anticipatory design scientist will periodically indulge in open-ended inquiry—serendipitously connecting mutually informative bodies of knowledge—and almost everybody uses Google as a mental prosthesis from time to time. But the amount of information in need of mental remixing far exceeds the amount of available mental space. There are not nearly enough comprehensive anticipatory design scientists to process the products of specialization. Equally important, autodidactic dilettantism is denigrated in our society of specialization. The solutions generated through comprehensive anticipatory design science are unlikely to attract the widespread support needed for comprehensive enactment.

Education is therefore an essential aspect of comprehensive anticipatory design science, not only in terms of committed design scientists' eclectic self-education, but also in terms of design science infiltrating the educational system, providing an alternative to specialized learning.[11] Everyone must be exposed to design science for design science to have the raw material and the influence to make a difference. The design scientist must be an educator as much as an innovator.

*Patterning*

Three hundred million years ago, Earth was a single landmass surrounded by ocean. The notion that the continents were once joined was first suggested by their matching contours, which implied to some nineteenth-century observers that the world was a colossal jigsaw puzzle cast asunder. In 1912, the German meteorologist Alfred Wegener organized the evidence into a theory, which he dubbed "continental drift." Geologists rejected it for the next fifty years, arguing that no earthly force could move continents such great distances.

Their skepticism was understandable. The drifting of continents—now universally accepted as plate tectonics—is far too gradual for humans to perceive. The same is true for other highly significant phenomena. When Charles Darwin first proposed natural selection, he faced at least as much resistance as Wegener; although his theory explained myriad observations, nobody had actually *seen* finches evolving. Likewise, the effects of our own collective activity—such as

---

11. Potential approaches to open-ended education are discussed at the end of Chapter 3.

climate change and loss of biodiversity—are almost invisible to us, because the impact spans the whole planet, growing over centuries. Like plate tectonics and evolution, the arrival of the Anthropocene epoch is not a human-scale phenomenon.

Buckminster Fuller conceived the Geoscope as a tool to help humans attain a global perspective, to see worldwide events and to probe geological time. It was to be an instrument for scoping Earth's patterns—an instrument of comprehensive anticipatory design science. And though it was never built adjacent to the United Nations, he always carried one in his head.

In order to anticipate comprehensively, the present-day design scientist must do as he did. Design scientists must be sensitive to natural patterns of change and human patterns of activity, extrapolating from fragmentary evidence. In the Anthropocene, these patterns will be interrelated. And since human activity is the driving force, they not only can be observed but also can be impacted.

However, patterns must be detected before they become settled, before the consequences are foregone conclusions. Unlike Wegener and Darwin, the design scientist cannot be passive.

There are now countless tools for scoping the planet. Microelectronic sensors are nearly ubiquitous, the Internet has made abundant data easy to access, and powerful computers and data visualization tools have given most everybody the ability to search for meaningful correlations. All that's required is curiosity and diligence.

To act on found patterns is more challenging. Global changes are too vast for any comprehensive anticipatory design scientist to make alone. For that reason, the design scientist must concentrate equally on communicating the patterns detected through design science, in order to encourage the global populace to re-pattern constructively.[12]

The comprehensive anticipatory design scientist is not only a designer of global systems, but also of global opinion. Both jobs are served by visualizing patterns.

## Efficiency

Every engineer esteems efficiency, the only universal value in engineering. The CPU of a computer, the engine in a car, and the plumbing for a city are all designed to be efficient. Yet efficiency is not a design specification in its own right. It must be specified in terms of function, and most engineered systems have many conflicting desiderata. The engineer seeks to optimize competing criteria—such as balancing the demands for high speed and low power consumption in a microprocessor.

Buckminster Fuller always optimized inventions in conventional engineering terms. His goal of "doing the most with the least"—a good definition of efficiency—was subsumed by functional considerations when he ceased lecturing and started building. For example, the geodesic domes designed for trade fairs balance weight of shipment against speed of assembly, considerations that certainly didn't inform the design of his proposed Dome over Manhattan.

But Fuller also considered efficiency in another way, which is rare in engineering and essential to comprehensive anticipatory design science. If conventional efficiency is *horizontal*—optimizing all the design requirements of a building or machine—design science also seeks *vertical*

---

12. Consider the potential of local geoscopes, as proposed at the end of Chapter 4.

efficiency: The artifact must be efficient not only for the maker, but also for society.

The comprehensive anticipatory design scientist has two sets of design specs that must intersect. A car engine must be designed to serve both the vehicle and the world as a whole; the optimal power source for automotive performance may be suboptimal for the performance of Spaceship Earth. While design science has already made inroads with high-performance electric cars such as the Tesla Roadster, comprehensive problem-solving requires that the designer ask whether vehicles should even be personal.

With so many criteria to balance—more than can ever realistically be enumerated—the comprehensive anticipatory design scientist risks never getting started, or reaching a solution so outlandish that society will never accept it. Both of these problems plagued the Manhattan Dome and many more of Fuller's most grandiose plans. But he was also practical. Domes got built, and some were impressively efficient on impressively many levels, even if they were imperfect.

No optimum is absolute. That is why pragmatism is also a desideratum of comprehensive anticipatory design science.[13] If a solution isn't implemented, it can never be efficient.

## Interaction

According to some accounts, the last person to have read everything was Immanuel Kant. Other historians attribute the achievement to John Milton or Erasmus of Rotterdam. But even if we attribute the achievement to the most recent claimant—Samuel Taylor Coleridge—universal knowledge

---

13. A pragmatic alternative to the Manhattan Dome is suggested at the end of Chapter 5.

was a thing of the past even when Buckminster Fuller was born in 1895. Comprehensivism simply isn't possible within a given head.

The eclecticism of an autodidactic education is one response to this problem. Guided by curiosity, serendipity can be a powerful mode of discovery. Every comprehensive anticipatory design scientist must learn in this way—at least as a supplement to formal education—just as every design scientist must master biomimesis, adaptability, patterning, and efficiency. But although all of these qualities are necessary for the comprehensive anticipatory design scientist, they are not sufficient for comprehensive anticipatory design science. Comprehensiveness must be collective.

Introducing comprehensivism into schools will help, as will the development of tools for widespread visualization of comprehensive patterns. However, the most important future development in comprehensive anticipatory design science will be the creation of new platforms for global interaction. All knowledge comes together when all minds come together. Given the right impetus, those minds might even envision a collective future.

Fuller conceived his World Game for just this purpose, recognizing that the free play of games might provide a framework for everyone to win. Even if his comprehension of game mechanics was weak, his intuition was right that games could bring humanity as close as humanly possible to the numinous universal optimum. Online games can fulfill and expand upon his vision.[14]

Design scientists can make these games using the design principles outlined here, though they'll be out of work if they succeed: The world gaming platform itself will be the

---

14. See the final section of Chapter 6 for more details.

ultimate comprehensive anticipatory design scientist. We should all be so fortunate.

## Coda:  Paper Architecture

WHEN CIVIL WAR struck Rwanda in 1990, the United Nations supplied metal bars and plastic tarp as materials for refugee shelters. But it didn't work out as expected. The metal was sold on the black market, and trees were chopped down to replace it, exacerbating wartime deforestation. For reasons nobody expected, the humanitarian aid was counterproductive.

Reading about the debacle, a young Japanese architect named Shigeru Ban proposed an alternative. Ban had been experimenting with cardboard tubes as a cheap material for temporary exhibits, and had found them to be remarkably strong and resilient. Since paper was less precious than metal, he reasoned that cardboard refugee shelters would be more economical—and less vulnerable to black market graft—than the standard UN shelters.

Following successful deployment in Rwanda, Ban's cardboard houses have been erected in disaster areas worldwide, from Kobe to Port-au-Prince to New Orleans. Ban has supplemented family dwellings with community centers and even a cardboard cathedral in Christchurch, New Zealand. With each catastrophe, he has further developed the structural potential of paper architecture. He has added strength by making walls curvy, and durability by adding waterproof coatings. He has exploited paper's translucency for natural light and personal privacy. His ingenuity has been recognized with museum exhibits and a Pritzker Prize. Yet Ban has not commercialized his cardboard architecture, nor has he proposed it as the future of building. On the contrary, he has continued making homes for private clients using more conventional materials.[15] "I like paper, but it's not the only material I use," he said in a 2013 *Japan Times* interview. "I use wood and steel and concrete too. The important thing is that the material must match the function."

Ban's paper architecture matches its function in myriad ways. As he surmised in Rwanda, cardboard is valuable in crises precisely because it has so little commercial value. Cardboard houses can be affordably erected and aren't worth stealing. Also cardboard is light enough to transport anywhere and to assemble by hand. And while the houses are strong, the fully recyclable materials psychologically suggest that refugee status is temporary, meaning that refugee camps are more likely to be accepted by neighboring communities, and refugees are less likely to be encamped permanently.

In other words, Ban's refugee shelters exemplify comprehensive anticipatory design science. Their design is comprehensive because they are completely adapted to their intended purpose, taking into account the physical needs of refugees, the resources of humanitarian organizations, and the sociopolitical reality of encampment. They are anticipatory because they are optimally designed for their entire life cycle, functioning physically, psychologically, and sociopolitically beyond the initial emergency. Their sturdiness anticipates the travails of refugee life, and their ephemerality anticipates refugees' reintegration into society.

Moreover, the shelters are comprehensively anticipatory in more global terms, because the kinds of emergencies they have served in the past are likely to grow more urgent in the future. Climate change is wreaking ever greater

---

15. Ban's residential and commercial commissions, always expensive and often lavish, support his *pro bono* humanitarian architectural practice.

environmental havoc. Natural disasters such as hurricanes are becoming more frequent. Equally perilous, unpredictable weather undermines farming, and scarcity of food undermines social stability. Catastrophe, famine, and warfare: These are the future conditions anticipated by Shigeru Ban's architecture. Addressing them with grace, his buildings make the immediate future endurable, giving society time for deeper amends.

Shigeru Ban often cites Buckminster Fuller as an influence on his work, though clearly Ban's vision differs considerably from that of Fuller (as well as Papanek and Google), and from the independent articulations suggested in these pages. His cardboard architecture is inspiring as evidence of what comprehensive anticipatory design science can achieve today when practiced creatively.

Comprehensive design benefits from profusion and variety, a truth Fuller recognized when he referred to himself as a *random element*. More comprehensive anticipatory design scientists are always needed. The obligation falls on everyone who belongs to the universe.

# FURTHER READING

## Selected Books by Buckminster Fuller

*4D Time Lock* (privately printed, 1928; reprint by Lama Foundation, 1972).

*And It Came to Pass—Not to Stay*, by R. Buckminster Fuller (Macmillan, 1976).

*Critical Path*, by R. Buckminster Fuller with Kiyoshi Kuromiya (St. Martin's Press, 1981).

*The Dymaxion World of Buckminster Fuller*, by R. Buckminster Fuller and Robert W. Marks (Anchor Press, 1960).

*Earth, Inc.*, by R. Buckminster Fuller (Anchor Press, 1973).

*Grunch of Giants*, by R. Buckminster Fuller (St. Martin's Press, 1983).

*Ideas and Integrities*, by R. Buckminster Fuller (Prentice Hall, 1963).

*Inventions: The Patented Works of R. Buckminster Fuller*, by R. Buckminster Fuller (St. Martin's Press, 1983).

*Nine Chains to the Moon*, by R. Buckminster Fuller (J. B. Lippincott, 1938).

*No More Secondhand God*, by R. Buckminster Fuller (Doubleday, 1963).

*Operating Manual for Spaceship Earth*, by R. Buckminster Fuller (E. P. Dutton, 1963).

*R. Buckminster Fuller on Education*, edited by Robert Kahn and Peter Wagschal (University of Massachusetts Press, 1979).

*Synergetics: Explorations in the Geometry of Thinking*, by R. Buckminster Fuller with E. J. Applewhite (Macmillan, 1975).

*Synergetics 2: Further Explorations in the Geometry of Thinking*, by R. Buckminster Fuller with E. J. Applewhite (Macmillan, 1979).

*Utopia or Oblivion*, by R. Buckminster Fuller (Bantam Books, 1969).

## Selected Books about Buckminster Fuller

*Becoming Bucky Fuller*, by Loretta Lorance (MIT Press, 2009).

*Buckminster Fuller*, by Martin Pawley (Taplinger, 1991).

*Buckminster Fuller: An Autobiographical Monologue/Scenario*, by Robert Snyder (St. Martin's Press, 1980).

*Buckminster Fuller: Anthology for the New Millennium*, by Thomas T. K. Zung (St. Martin's Press, 2001).

*Buckminster Fuller: At Home in the Universe*, by Alden Hatch (Crown, 1974).

*Buckminster Fuller: Dymaxion Car*, by Jonathan Glancey (Ivory Press, 2013).

*Buckminster Fuller: Starting with the Universe*, edited by Michael Hays and Dana Miller (Yale University Press, 2008).

*Buckminster Fuller's Universe: An Appreciation*, by Lloyd Steven Sieden (Plenum Press, 1989).

*Bucky: A Guided Tour of Buckminster Fuller*, by Hugh Kenner (William Morrow, 1973).

*Bucky Works: Buckminster Fuller's Ideas for Today*, by J. Baldwin (John Wiley & Sons, 1996).

*Fuller Houses: R. Buckminster Fuller's Dymaxion Dwellings and Other Domestic Adventures*, by Federico Neder (Lars Müller, 2008).

*New Views on R. Buckminster Fuller*, edited By Hsiao-Yun Chu and Roberto G. Trujillo (Stanford University Press, 2009).

*Pilot for Spaceship Earth*, by Athena V. Lord (Macmillan, 1978).

*R. Buckminster Fuller*, by John McHale (George Brazillier, 1962).

*Wizard of the Dome: R. Buckminster Fuller, Designer for the Future*, by Sidney Rosen (Little, Brown, 1969).

*Your Private Sky: R. Buckminster Fuller—The Art of Design Science*, edited by Joachim Krausse and Claude Lichtenstein (Lars Müller, 1999).

*Your Private Sky: R. Buckminster Fuller—Discourse*, edited by Joachim Krausse and Claude Lichtenstein (Lars Müller, 2001).

# INDEX

ABC, 75n5
Abu Dhabi, 122–124
Adaptability, 178–180
Additive manufacturing software
    and hardware, 66–68, 89n14
AEG, 50–51, 53
Aerodynamics, 32–35, 33n2
Afghanistan, 16
Agarwal, Anant, 71–72, 79, 80
Agnefjäll, Peter, 48
AIA. *See* American Institute of
    Architects
Air Ocean World Town, 43
Alaska and Eskimo village,
    169–170
Al Jaber, Ahmed, 124
American Institute of Architects
    (AIA), 11, 17, 18, 58, 58n13
American Standard Sanitary
    Manufacturing Company, 11
*America's Army* (military training
    MMO), 160
Anthropocene epoch, 183
Anticipatory design science, 2–3,
    20, 172, 178–179, 181–185
Architects and architecture. *See also*
    Housing
    Fuller's housing designs.
    *See* Dymaxion housing;
    4D House
    Fuller's work at father-in-law's
    business, 10, 11, 56

modern architecture, Le
    Corbusier's view of, 52
    reaction to 4D House, 11, 18
    Softkill Design, 66–67
Architectural League of
    New York, 11
Armi, C. Edson, 33n2
Armour & Company, 7–8, 13
Artificial intelligence, 40n9
Asawa, Ruth, 88
Audi, 34
Autodesk, 89
Autodidactic learning, 78, 82,
    86–88, 181, 186
Automobile industry, 12–13, 29–46.
    *See also* Dymaxion car; *specific*
    *manufacturers*
    aerodynamic design, 32–35
    automobile design, Fuller's
    critique of, 32, 32n1
    autoplane prototype, 42
    chassis construction, 40
    nature as inspiration for, 37–40
Autoplane prototype, 42
Avalon Hill (gaming company),
    156, 157
Avion-Automobile, 42

Ban, Shigeru, 187–189, 188n15
Bartle, Richard, 157
Bauhaus, 53, 54, 57, 57n11
*Baukasten im Großen*, 53–54

Bear Island, Maine, 5–6
Beech Aircraft Company, 14,
    49, 62, 64
Behrens, Peter, 50–51
Behrman, Walter, 94n1
Beijing, air pollution in, 118n4
Beistegui, Charles de, 53
Benyus, Janine, 41
Benz, Henry, 33
Biomimesis/biomimicry, 36–37, 39,
    40–41, 42n10, 116, 176–178
Bionic Car, 36, 39, 40
Black Mountain College, 15, 73,
    82–83, 84, 86–87
Bloomfield, Lincoln, 146, 146n8,
    155–156
Board of Economic Warfare, 14
BOGSAT, 145n7
BoKlok house, 48, 55n5
Bolinas (California), 164–165
Bombrini, Riparo, 55n6
Brain, study of, 110–111
Brand, Stewart, 81, 129n16
Brandt, Willy, 93
Brasília, 128
Breer, Carl, 34, 38
Brockmann, Dirk, 112, 112n21
Buckminster Fuller Institute,
    104, 104n12
Bundy, McGeorge, 135n1
Bundy, William, 135n1
Bungling Bay (gaming
    company), 157
Burgess, Starling, 39

Cage, John, 83n10
Cahill, Bernard J. S.,
    103–104, 103n10
Caniff, Milton, 136n2
Caproni, Gianni, 52
Cardboard houses, 187–189
Cash movement, U.S. states redrawn
    according to, 112, 112n21

Cayley, George, 37, 39, 46, 177
CBS, 73–74, 75
Chandigarh, 128
Chassis construction, 40
Chaturgana (Indian form of chess),
    138, 156
Chess, 138–139
Chicago Institute of Design, 84
China
    model city plans in, 128n15
    war games, 138
Chrysler Airflow, 34, 35, 35n4, 38
Chu & Trujillo, eds.: New Views on
    R. Buckminster Fuller, 19n4
Ciphering, 83
Cities. See Domed cities; Ecocities;
    Urban population
Civilization (game), 157n17
Clarke, Arthur C., 168
Clark Mansion (New York
    City), 56n8
Climate change, 115–117. See also
    Environment
CNC machines, 65
Coefficient of drag (Cd), 34, 36
Cohen, Harold, 71
Cohesiveness, 177–178
Cold War, 64, 70, 134
    war games and, 143–144
Coleridge, Samuel Taylor, 185
Commerce Department, U.S., 16
Comprehensive anticipatory
    design science. See
    Anticipatory design science
Comprehensivism, 20,
    177–178, 186
Continental Classroom (television
    show), 74, 75n4, 81
Convergence, 13, 180–182
Cooper-Hewitt National Design
    Museum, 173
Copper mining, 148
Corb. See Le Corbusier

Cornell University's School of
    Architecture, 107
Corporations
    environmental initiatives
        and, 175
    nature of, 175
    war-gaming, use of, 156n15
Counterculture, 17
Coursera, 79
Cox, David, 91
Crosthwaite & Gardiner, 30
Cuboctahedron, 95, 104,
    104n11, 105
Cunningham, Merce, 83n10
Curiosity, 88–92, 186
Curtiss, Glenn, 42

Daimler, 40, 67n22. *See also*
    Mercedes-Benz
DaimlerChrysler Innovation
    Symposium (2005), 36
Darwin, Charles, 182
Defense Advanced Research
    Projects Agency
    (DARPA), 89
de Kooning, Elaine, 83
de Kooning, Willem, 83n10
Delage, Louis, 52
Desovereignization, 150
Dini, Enrico, 66
Dirigibles, 37
Discovery Channel's *Mega
    Engineering* series, 121
Disease maps, 98, 99, 99n5
Domed cities, 118–122, 118nn4–5
    climate control in, 131
    Houston proposal, 121–122
    Manhattan proposal, 118–119,
        127, 174, 185
    as microclimate, 130–131
    Winooski (Vermont) proposal,
        120–121
Dominis, John, 164

Drexler, Arthur, 87n11, 119
Durer, Albrecht, 102
Dymaxion car, 12–13, 18,
    29–46, 177
    disposition of prototypes (cars
        1–3), 29–30
    Dymaxion Car No. 4 (Foster's
        recreation), 30–31
    as 4D transportation unit,
        41, 57n10
    hybrid nature of, 41–42
    logo, 37
    nature as inspiration for, 37–39,
        37n7. *See also* Biomimesis/
        biomimicry
    problems with, 31, 35, 35n5
Dymaxion Chronofile
    archive of, 3n1, 19n4
    creation of, 3
    influences on Fuller revealed
        in, 57n11
Dymaxion Corporation
    (Bridgeport,
    Connecticut), 12–13
Dymaxion Deployment Units,
    13, 61–63
Dymaxion housing (Dwelling
    Machine), 11, 14, 179
    climate control, 60, 60n15, 63
    funding for prototype, 61
    Graham's modifications, 49, 64
    inadaptability of, 64
    industrialized construction of, 57
    New York Architectural
        League presentation
        (1929), 59–60
    patent applications, 58, 58n13
    streamlining, 60
    suspension system, 57, 57n12,
        59, 63, 86
    transportable, 57, 60, 148
    Wichita House, 48–49, 50, 53n4,
        55–65, 180

Dymaxion maps, 14, 95, 100–106
  Buckminster Fuller Institute
    competition (2013), 104, 104n12
  geodesics and, 106–107
  interaction possibilities, 104, 105
  "Mercator World," 97
  *One Ocean World Town Plan*, 100
  polar perspective of,
    101–102, 104
  Van Wijk's myriahedra
    compared to, 105
  world peace game and, 136, 151

*Early X-Piece* (sculpture), 86
Ecocities, 122–127
Ecosystem, human, 43–46
Educational ideas, 70–92, 182n11
  autodidactic learning, 78, 82,
    86–88, 181, 186
  curiosity, cultivation of, 88–92
  educational television, 73–78
  Fuller's lectures, 81–88
  life-long schooling, 76
  Massive Open Online Courses
    (MOOCs), 72, 78–81,
    89–91, 89n13
  obsolescence of schools, 71
  paradoxical thinking of
    Fuller on, 88
  SIU documentary of
    Fuller, 70–71
  social networking among
    students, 79–80
edX, 79, 91
Efficiency, 6, 10, 11–15, 77n7, 184–185
  in aerodynamic design, 32,
    34, 36, 37
  of automation, 72, 76
  and design science, 176
  "doing more with less," 63, 184
  of geodesic domes, 119

  in housing design, 60, 63, 174
  societal, 78
  technological, 147, 149, 175
  urban, 119, 126, 155
  world game and, 154
Electricity and energy
  consumption, 117, 151, 170
Electronic Arts, 160
"Energy slaves," 101
Environment, 115–133
  Abu Dhabi initiatives, 122–124
  climate change, 115–117
  domed cities and, 118–122,
    118nn4–5, 130–131. *See also*
    Domed cities
  ecocities, 122–127
  geoengineering and,
    115–117, 116n2
  geothermal heat exchangers,
    131–132
  Google Nest and, 174
  Green Floats (marine cities),
    125–127
  green technology, 41
  metroengineering, 129–133
  naleds, use of, 130
  Winooski, Vermont, proposed
    dome, 120–121
Ephemeralization, 16, 133
Erasmus of Rotterdam, 185
Eslan Institute, 164
ETC Group, 115, 116n1, 116n3
Ethylene tetrafluoroethylene
  (ETFE), 121
Eurocentrism, 93
European Modernism. *See*
  Modernism
*EverQuest* (multiplayer online
  game), 158
Exploratory Data Analysis, 110n16
Expo 67. *See* Montreal's Expo 67

Factory-produced housing. *See* Industrialized housing
Factory work, 7, 14
Fadell, Tony, 175
Farnsworth, Philo T., 60n16
Farnsworth House, 54
*Flag* paintings (Johns), 110
Flisvos Park (Athens), 131
Floating cities, 125–126, 125n12
Floating compression, 86–87
Florida, 126
Ford, Henry, 33, 46, 51, 147, 175
Ford Motor Corporation, 15
    Lincoln Zephyr, 34–35, 35n4
    Model A, 33, 35, 57, 61, 61n17
    Model T, 33, 34, 51
*Fortune* magazine, 13, 49, 49n1, 53n4, 62, 62n20, 101, 148–149, 148n10
Foster, Norman, 30–31, 123
4D House, 10–11, 18. *See also* Dymaxion housing
France
    cartographers, 99, 100n6
    German war planning against, 141–142
Free war games, 140–141, 142, 144, 145n7
Fuller, Alexandra (daughter), 9
Fuller, Allegra (daughter), 10, 31
Fuller, Anne (wife), 8–9, 17–18, 167–168
Fuller, Buckminster ("Bucky").
    *See also* Dymaxion; Fuller, Buckminster, writings of; Geodesics; World Game
    as anticipatory design scientist, 2–3
    as autodidact, 181
    college education, 6–7, 9, 18
    crafting his own personal myth, 2–4, 18–20, 42, 58n13

cult status of, 20, 24, 81–82, 167
death of, 18, 168
"doing more with less," 63, 184
educational television and. *See* Television
efficiency and, 184–186
eyesight of, 5
family and childhood background, 5–6
futuristic ideas of, 13, 17
honors given to, 17
inconsistency of, 4, 78, 88, 104n11, 167, 176
influence of, 22, 86–88, 168, 189
Le Corbusier's influence on, 55–56, 59
legacy of, 168–169
map making by, 94. *See also* Dymaxion map; Geoscope
marriage, 8–9
nonteaching jobs of, 7–8, 10, 11, 14, 49, 56
obituaries, 18
obsessiveness and megalomania of, 49, 88
Papanek and, 168–173, 168n2
personal transformation (1927), 2–3, 10
proselytizing, 2, 3, 18, 81–82, 119, 169n3. *See also* Lectures and seminars by Fuller
as random element, 189
suicide attempt, 2, 4, 10
teaching and educational positions held by, 73, 152, 152n12. *See also* Black Mountain College; Harvard University; Lectures and seminars by Fuller; MIT; Southern Illinois University

Fuller, Buckminster, writings of
   *American Neptune* article
      (1944), 43
   "The Case for a Domed City"
      article (1965), 119
   *Critical Path*, 77, 96, 108–109,
      127, 150
   *The Dymaxion World of
      Buckminster Fuller*, 118
   *Education Automation*, 75, 82, 88,
      88n12, 133
   *Emergent Humanity* (essay), 88–89
   *Everything I Know* (lecture 1975),
      37, 42n10, 147
   *4D Time Lock*, 11, 58, 100–101
   *How It Came About (World
      Game)*, 136, 153
   *Nine Chains to the Moon*, 13,
      64n21, 69
   *Operating Manual for Spaceship
      Earth*, 43, 113
   *Portfolio & Art News Annual*
      article (1961), 87
   *Utopia or Oblivion*, 150
   *World Game Series: Document
      One*, 152
Fuller, Richard Buckminster, Sr.
   (father), 6
Fuller Houses, Inc., 49
*Fundamentals of Neuroscience*
   (MOOC course), 91

Gall, James, 94
Gaming and game theory, 137, 145,
   145n6, 186–187. *See also* God
   games; War games
   World Game, 136–137, 152–156,
      160–162, 186
Gaty, John, 64
General Motors, 40
Geodesics, 14–16, 17, 18

automated cotton mill inside
   dome, 85–86
bamboo domes, 85
Black Mountain dome
   construction, 83–84
brand name of "geodesic
   dome," 106n13
dymaxion maps and, 106–107
first large-scale domes, 83,
   118–119
Kahn's critique of, 165–167
Pentagon, dome
   constructed at, 84
photographs of geodesic
   domes, 164
Geoengineering, 115–117, 116n2
Geological maps, 98
Geologists, 182
Geoscope, 95, 107–109, 111, 113,
   136n3, 174, 183. *See also*
   Dymaxion maps
Geothermal heat exchangers,
   131–132
German use of war games, 139–142
Glancey, Jonathan, 31
Gliders, 39, 40
Global Energy Network
   Institute, 155n14
Global online marketplace, 46
God games, 157, 157n17, 160–161
Goode, John Paul, 94n1
Goodyear, 62n19
Google, 181
   acquisition of Nest Labs,
      173–175
   Public Data Explorer, 113
   SketchUp, 65
Graham, William, 49, 64
Greek war games, 138
Green Floats (marine cities),
   125–127

Greenhouse gases, 116–117
Green technology, 41
Gropius, Walter, 50–51, 53, 54, 55,
    57n11, 65
    "Programme for the
        Establishment of a Company
        for the Provision of Housing
        on Aesthetically Consistent
        Principles," 50
Gulf of Tonkin Resolution
    (1964), 135

Habitat (virtual world), 159
Halley, Edmond, 97–98
Happiness map, 112
Harper College (Illinois), 131n18
Harrah, Bill, 29–30
Harvard University
    Fuller's undergraduate time at,
        6–7, 18
    Fuller teaching at, 73
    honors from, 17
    partnering with MIT on free
        online curriculum, 72
    speaking at, 11
Hatred, map of, 112
Haussmann, Georges-Eugène, 122
Henry Ford Museum, 50
Hewlett, Anne, 8–9. See also
    Fuller, Anne
Hewlett, James Monroe, 10
Hewlett Packard, 89, 91
Housing. See also Dymaxion housing
    adaptability of 3D computer
        design, 65–68
    additive manufacturing software
        and hardware, 66–68, 89n14
    BoKlok house, 48, 55n5
    cardboard houses, 187–189
    climate control, 60,
        60n15, 63, 67

Farnsworth House, 54
Flanders housing shortage, 51
4D House, 10–11, 18. See also
    Dymaxion housing
    Gropius's view of, 50–51, 53
    Ikea, 47–48, 50, 68
    industrialized, 51, 54, 57
    Le Corbusier's view of, 51–53
    Maison Citrohan, 51, 53
    Maison Dom-ino, 51–52, 54
    post–World War II shortage, 64
    repro-shelters, 67, 69
    spacecraft as, 131n19
    Suspension Houses
        Project, 57n12
    transportable, 43, 55, 57, 60
    Tugendhat House, 54
    WikiHouses, 65–67
Houston, proposed as domed city,
    121–122
Human Brain Project, 111, 113
Human ecosystem, 43–46
Humanitarian aid, 187
Humboldt, Alexander von, 98–99
Humboldt State University, 112

Icosahedron, 104, 104n11, 105, 106,
    107, 110
Ikea, 47–48, 50, 55n5, 68
Indonesia, 170–171
Industrial Designers Society of
    America, 173
Industrialization of United States,
    148–149
Industrialized housing, 51, 54, 57
Infographics, 96, 96nn2–3, 104n12
Information visualization, 110–111,
    110n16, 113–114
Integration of technologies, 63
Interaction, 185–187
International Style, 54

Internet, potential of, 181, 183. *See also* Online
Invention as convergence, 13

*Jamais Contente* (Jenatzy's car design), 32
Japan
    bullet trains, 36–37
    Kamikaze missions and, 143
    war games, use of, 142
Jaray, Paul, 33–34, 35n3
Jenatzy, Camille, 32, 33
Jets, 42, 42n10
Johns, Jasper, 109–110

Kahn, Herman, 143, 144n4
Kahn, Lloyd, 164–166, 167n1, 168
    denunciation of Fuller, 165–167
    *Domebooks*, 164–165
    *Refried Domes*, 166
    *Smart But Not Wise*, 165
Kaiser Aluminum, 175
Kamprad, Ingvar, 47, 68
Kant, Immanuel, 185
Kennedy, Robert, 146
Kenner, Hugh, 18, 20, 42, 152n12
    *Bucky*, 19
Keyes, Gene, 103n10
Khan Academy, 89n13
Khoshnevis, Behrokh, 66
Khrushchev, Nikita, 16
Kiribati, 126, 126n13
Koller, Daphne, 79
*Kriegsspiel* (Prussian war game), 139–141, 145, 156, 157

Lambert, Johann Heinrich, 94, 94n1
Laser technology, 76n6
Lavey, John, 112
Le Corbusier, 49, 53n4, 55n6, 59, 65

influence on Fuller, 55–56, 59
    Maison Dom-ino, 51–53
    *Toward an Architecture*, 48, 52, 55, 61n18
Lectures and seminars by Fuller, 2, 17, 18, 32, 37, 59–60, 73, 81–88, 90, 108, 131n18, 152, 152n12, 164, 167
Ledwinka, Hans, 35n3
Legacy, 163–189
Lemay, Curtis, 135n1
le Nautonier, Guillaume, 97–98
Liebeskind, Daniel, 55n5
*Life* magazine, 49n1, 95, 97, 102, 164, 166
Living PlanIT, 124, 124n11
Lorance, Loretta: *Becoming Bucky Fuller*, 19n4, 56n7
Lord, Athena, 42
Luce, Henry, 148n10

Maison Citrohan, 51, 53
Maison Dom-ino, 51–52, 54
Makerspace, 89–90, 90n16
Malthus, Thomas, 6
Malthusianism, 6, 8, 9, 70
Maps, 93–114. *See also* Dymaxion map; Geoscope
    Cahill's map, 103–104, 103n10
    cash movement, states redrawn according to, 112, 112n21
    disease maps, 98, 99, 99n5
    European statistical atlases, 99–100
    French cartographers, 99, 100n6
    geological maps, 98
    global voyaging and, 97–98
    happiness map, 112
    hatred, map of, 112
    Johns's *Map*, 109–110
    Mercator's navigation map, 93, 103, 105

"Mercator World," 97
meteorological maps, 98
multidimensional approach to, 96
myriahedral projection, 105
Peters's world map, 93–96,
    104n12, 108
*The Statistical Atlas of the Ninth
    Census* (U.S. 1870), 100
thematic maps, 99–100
UN standard map, 93–94
Van Wijk's myriahedra, 105
water supply (U.S.), 112
WNYC's U.S. median income
    map (2011), 111
*World Energy Map*, 101
Marks, Robert: *The Dymaxion
    World of Buckminster Fuller*,
    32n1, 46
Marshall Field's department
    store, 11, 59
Marshall Islands, 126
Masdar (proposed UAE city),
    123–125, 124nn9–10, 128
Masdar Institute of Science and
    Technology, 124
Massive Open Online Courses
    (MOOCs), 72, 78–81,
    89–91, 89n13
McCone, John, 135n1
McGill University
    (Montreal), 84–85
McGonigal, Jane: *Reality Is Broken*,
    159, 160n18
McNamara, Robert, 135
*Meet the Professor* (television
    show), 75n5
"Mega-City Pyramid" concept,
    127, 127n14
*Mega Engineering* series (television
    show), 121
Meier, Richard, 55n5

Meier, Sid, 157n17
Mendeleev, Dmitri, 98n4
Mercator, Gerardus, navigation
    map of, 93, 103, 105, 114
"Mercator World," 97
Mercedes-Benz, 34, 36, 37, 40
Metabolist movement, 125n12
Meteorological maps, 98
Metroengineering, 129–133
Meyer, Adolf, 53, 55
Mezes, Theodore, 29, 31
Microclimates, 130–131
Mies van der Rohe, Ludwig, 49,
    54, 55, 57n11, 63
Military
    Dymaxion Deployment Units
        designed for, 61–63
    game technology licensed
        by, 160n19
    gaming Vietnam, 134–137
    geodesic domes, use of, 16
    Naval Academy education, 9
    service in Navy, 9, 13
    war games and game theory,
        134–137
    web development linked to, 178n8
Miller, Marilyn, 7
Milton, John, 185
Milton, Massachusetts, 4
MIT, 71–72, 73
Mobility. *See* Automobile industry;
    Dymaxion car
Modernism, 48–50, 53, 54, 56, 63,
    64, 69, 70
Moltke, Helmuth von, 140, 143
Mongolia, 129–130
Montreal's Expo 67, 16, 109, 109n15,
    120, 136, 136n3, 146, 162
MOOCs. *See* Massive Open
    Online Courses
Moral statistics, 99

Mosteller, Charles F., 75
Multiplayer online games
    (MMOs), 158–160
*Multi-User Dungeon (MUD)*,
    157–158
Mumford, Lewis: *The Pentagon of
    Power*, 127–129
Museum of Modern Art
    architectural symposium
    (1948), 49
    Fuller exhibition, 87n11
    Manhattan skybreak picture in
    exhibit (1959), 118
Myriahedra, 105
Myth of Buckminster Fuller, 2–4,
    18–20, 42, 58n13

Naleds, 130
National Automobile Museum, 30
National Center for Atmospheric
    Research, 117
Nature as inspiration, 37–39, 37n7,
    42–45, 42n10, 177–178. *See
    also* Biomimesis/biomimicry
Naval Academy (Annapolis), 9
Naval Electronic War Simulator,
    145, 152
Naval War College, 141, 145, 146
Navy, service in, 9, 13
NBC, 74, 75, 75n4
Nelson, George, 49–50
Nest Labs, 173
New York Architectural
    League, 59–60
New York City
    Fuller's East River plans, 113
    Manhattan Dome, 118–119, 127,
    174, 185
New York University, 74
Ng, Andrew, 79
Nimitz, Chester, 143

Nomura Securities, 125
North Carolina State College, 85

Octet truss, 16
Online curriculum of college
    classes, 71–72
Online virtual worlds and games,
    158–159, 186–187. *See also*
    Gaming and game theory

Pan-American Aeronautical
    Exposition (1917), 42
Papanek, Victor, 168–173, 168n2,
    170n2, 175
    *Design for the Real World*, 168,
    169, 171–172
Paris (France), 122
Paris Air Salon (1921), 42
Parkes, Edmund A., 99n5
Patterning, 182–184
Pawley, Martin: *Buckminster
    Fuller*, 49n2
Peace, 70, 134–162
    Bloomfield's peace games, 146n8
    Fuller's peace-game thinking,
    147–148
    funding sought by Fuller for
    world-gaming, 152–153
    war games and game theory,
    134–146
    world peace game, Fuller's plan
    for, 136–137
Penn, Arthur, 84
Periodic table of the
    elements, 98n4
Peters, Arno, 93–94, 95, 96,
    104n12, 108
Phelps Dodge Corporation,
    101, 148
Planetariums, 107, 107n14
Planned cities, 127–129

Planning. *See* Maps
Politics
    anti-political rhetoric in world
        peace games, 149–150
    Cold War, 70
    disconnect with constituents, 75
    Vietnam War and, 85
"Pollution domes," 118n4
Polyhedron, 102
Porsche, Ferdinand, 35, 35n3
Portugal, proposed ecocity in, 124
Postmodernism, 50
Presidential Medal of Freedom, 17
Princeton University, 87
Pritzker Prize, 187
Projection, 94n1

Quebec, 7

Racing cars, 32–33
Radicalism, 60
Radio communication, 9, 170–171
RAND Corporation, 137, 144
Random element, 189
Rasch, Heinz and Bodo, 57n12
Reagan, Ronald, 17
Refugee shelters, 187–189
Reisswitz, Georg von, 139–140,
    141, 145, 156
Renaissance, 97
Repro-shelters, 67
Resource cycling, 46, 178n9
Roberts, Charles, 156
Robinson, Arthur, 94n1
Romany Marie's (Greenwich
    Village tavern), 11, 59
Rwanda civil war, 187–188
Rybczynski, Witold, 50n3

Sadao, Shoji, 86
Samsung, 175

San Francisco, 122
Schelling, Thomas, 146
    *The Strategy of Conflict*, 144
Sculthorpe Airfield experiment,
    115–116
Seagram Building (New York
    City), 70, 91
*Second Life* (online game),
    158–159, 160
Seldes, Gilbert, 73
    "The 'Errors' of Television"
        article, 73n2
Self-organizing society, 43
Senate Subcommittee on
    Intergovernmental Relations
        (1969), 137, 155
Serendipity, 186
Shelter. *See* Dymaxion housing;
    Housing
*Shelter* magazine, 12, 61n18
Shimizu Corporation, 125–126,
    127, 127n14
Shoriki, Matsutaro, 127
Siberia, 130
Sieden, Lloyd Steven, 32n1, 37n7
    *Buckminster Fuller: An
        Appreciation* (Sieden), 32n1
Sigma I and II war games,
    135n1, 136n2
Silver, Aaron, 67
*SimCity* (game), 157, 160, 161
*SimEarth* (game), 157
SIU. *See* Southern Illinois University
Slime molds, 44–45
Snelson, Kenneth, 86–87, 87n11
Snow, John, 99, 99n5, 102n9
Social media, 113
    networking among
        students, 79–80
Softkill Design, 66–67, 67n22
Soft Kill Option (SKO) software, 40

Solar radiation management
    (SRM), 116–117
Soleri, Paolo, 172n7
Songdo (South Korea), 128
Sonoran Institute, 112
Southern Illinois University (SIU),
    16, 70, 71n1, 75–76, 77n7,
    82–85, 108
Soviet Union, 16, 144. *See also*
    Cold War
Spaceship Earth, 15, 19, 21–25, 90,
    96, 108, 150, 185
Specialization, 180–181
SpikerBox, 91
*Spore* (game), 157
Squatter cities, 129n16
Stager, Gary, 90n16
Stanley, Francis and Freelan, 32–33
State Natural History Museum
    (Stuttgart), 36
*The Statistical Atlas of the Ninth
    Census* (U.S. 1870), 100
Stockade Building Systems,
    10, 11, 56
Stratospheric Particle Injection for
    Climate Engineering Project,
    115–116
Streamlining, 33–35, 60
*Sunrise Semester* (television show),
    74, 75n4, 81
Suspension Houses Project, 57n12
Synergy, 15

Taichung Gateway Park
    (Taiwan), 131
Tailorcraft, 62n19
Takeuchi, Masayuki, 126
Tampier, René, 42
Tatra T77, 34, 35, 35n3
TED Talk
    Agarwal (2013), 71
    Benyus (2005), 41

Television, 60n16
    educational television, 73–78
    two-way television, 24, 71,
    72, 75–76, 76n6, 77, 81,
    170n6, 181
Tensegrity, 16, 87
Tetra City proposal,
    127–128, 127n14
Tetrahedra, 5, 16, 17, 127
Thematic maps, 99–100
Thermochromic tile, 132
Third industrial revolution, 89,
    90n16, 91
Thomas Schelling explored the
    possibility in a book called
    *The Strategy of Conflict*, 144
Thompson, D'Arcy
    Wentworth: *On Growth and
    Form*, 38
Thorpe, Jonathan, 128–129
3D computer design, 65–68,
    90, 111
Thrun, Sebastian, 78, 80
*Time* magazine, 60–61
Tjaarda, John, 34–35
Tong, Anote, 126
Torpedo tourer, 33
Total War Research Institute
    (Japan), 142
Toyota Prius, 35
Trademarking of WORLD
    GAME, 152
Transportation. *See* Automobile
    industry; Dymaxion car
Trubshaw, Roy, 157
Tugendhat House, 54
Tukey, John, 110n16
Tuul River, 129–130
Tuvalu, 126
Twitter, 112
Two-way television, 24, 71, 72, 75–76,
    76n6, 77, 81, 170n6, 181

Udacity, 79, 80–81
*Ultima Online* (multiplayer online
    game), 159
UNICEF, 94
Union Tank Car Company, 16
United Arab Emirates (UAE),
    122–124
United Nations, 93–94, 95,
    108–109, 161, 183, 187
United States Information Agency
    (USIA), 109, 135–136, 150
University of Athens, 131
University of Michigan, 84
University of Minnesota, 87
University of Southern
    California, 66
University of Vermont, 112
Urban heat island effect, 130n17
Urban population, 117, 128–129. *See
    also* Domed cities; Ecocities
    metroengineering and, 129–133
    in squatter cities, 129n16
Utopia, 150n11

Vance, Cyrus, 135n1
van Creveld,
    Martin: *Wargames*, 135n1
van Wijk, Jarke J., 105
*Variety*, 177–178
Verdy du Vernois, Julius von,
    140–141
Vietnam War, 85, 135
    gaming and, 134–137, 135n1
Violence in virtual worlds, 159
Virtual worlds, 158–162
Volkswagen Beetle, 35
Von Neumann, John, 137, 144n4
    *Theory of Games and Economic
        Behavior* (with Morgenstern), 144

War games, 134–146
    choice-points in, 155–156

compromise as element of, 154
corporate war-gaming, 156n15
free war games, 140–141
*kriegsspiel* (Prussian), 139–141
non-military implications of
    military actions as factor in, 142
*Raid on Bungling Bay* (civilian
    game), 156
recreational war-gaming
    industry, 156–157
Sigma I and II, 135n1, 136n2
successful use of, 142
*Tactics* (civilian game), 156
Vietnam and, 134–137
Warren, Waldo, 60n14
Washington University (St.
    Louis), 84
Watson, Matthew, 116n2
Weber, Thomas, 36, 37
Wegener, Alfred, 182
Wells, H. G.: *Little Wars*, 156n16
Wheeler, Earl, 135n1
White, Harvey E., 74, 75
*Whole Earth Catalog*, 81
Wichita House, 48–49, 50, 53n4,
    55–65, 180
WikiHouses, 65–67
Wikipedia, 181
Windcatcher, 123
Wind patterns, 98, 125
Wind resistance, 31, 32–34
Winooski, Vermont, 120–121
WNYC's U.S. median income
    map (2011), 111
World Game, Fuller's plan for,
    136–137, 152–156, 186
    as alternative to voting, 162
    potential for, 160–162
    shortcomings of,
        154–156, 155n14
*World of Warcraft* (multiplayer
    online game), 158–159

World Resources Inventory, 149, 151

World's Fair (1933), 13, 61

World's Fair (1964), 119

World's Fair (1967). *See* Montreal's Expo 67

World War I, 9, 16, 133, 141–142

World War II, 13, 61
  war games, use of, 142–144

World Wide Web, 178

*World Without Oil* (online game), 159–160

Wright, Frank Lloyd, 118, 168, 169n4

Wright, Orville, 34

Wright, Will, 156–157, 160

Wright Brothers, 39, 55, 55n6

Wyatt, Wilson, 62

Ydholm, Mikael, 48

Youngblood, Gene, 152

Zeppelin, 43, 57

Zimbabwe construction, 37

Zoomobiles, 42–43, 46, 177

Zulli, Floyd, Jr., 74, 77

Zung, Thomas T. K., 121

Self-MYTHS > 4 † danced 8 >
8 - Spheres X Forces

Tetraheda
Houses
5 | 14
10 Future = Plastics
13 Bin Houses
15 Geodesic Dome
1948 (16)

DYMAXION = Houses/cars
Map 14

12. Future
car - 3 Wheels

13 - ahead
of his
Time